Current Issues in Indian Shipping

Current Issues in Indian Shipping

H. B. Desai
Former Director
Indian Institute of Foreign Trade
New Delhi

Commonwealth Publishers
New Delhi (India)

Edition 2025

ISBN 81-7169-014-9

Published by
COMMONWEALTH PUBLISHERS (P) LTD.
4831/24, Govind Lane,
Ansari Road, Darya Ganj,
New Delhi - 110002
Ph. : 23272541, 23242541
e-mail : commonwealthpublishers2016@gmail.com

Distributed by :
ARJUN PUBLISHING HOUSE
4831/24, Govind Lane,
Ansari Road, Darya Ganj,
New Delhi - 110002
Ph. : 23272541, 23242541
e-mail : arjunbooks2001@gmail.com

Laser Typesetting by :
Dimple Computers
Delhi

Printed at :
Milan Enterprises
Delhi

Dedicated to the
Memory of my Father
Whose Missionary Zeal Continues
To Inspire Me?

PREFACE

THIS Publication constitutes a companion volume to my previous book entitled "Indian Shipping Perspectives" brought out towards the end of 1989. It deals with current issues in Indian Shipping and represents collections of my articles written in the Perspective Column of the Marine Times; since beginning of 1988 to April, 1989. Encouraged by the appreciative response to the first publication, the publishers have ventured to bring out the second volume for keeping abreast the interested business executives, academicians, students, professional and policy formulators in the Government, with new developments and topical issues concerning international trade and shipping. It may be of special interest to journalists associated with business dailies which appear to be evincing greater interest in the subject than in the past. In the context of the on going, current exercise an formulation of our Eighth Five Year Plan, the issues dealt with in this publication, acquire added importance. Although the problems of Indian shipping are welknown, conceptualisation of these problems still represents an area of Terna Incognita. As a matter of fact to many, it is an area of total darkness. The author's endeavours have been to bring them, atleast in the two light zone.

H.B. DESAI

April, 1989
New Delhi.

CONTENTS

1

PORT SERVICES
PRIVATISATION AS PANACEA

In The context of the growing importance of foreign trade in general and exports in particular, the crucial role of the available facilities at Indian seaports cannot be overemphasised. Our port system and sub-system consist of ten major ports, five on the west coast of India (Kandla, Bombay, Marmugoa, New Mangalore and Cochin) and five on the east coast (Calcutta-Haldia, Paradeep, Vishakapatnam, Madras and New Tuticorin), Nhava Shiva, across the Bombay harbour, and expected to be functional in 1989 will be the eleventh major port of the country. Besides, there are numerous intermediate and minor ports, over 150, located on our vast coastline measuring 5,000 kms.

Administratively the major ports are under the central government which is responsible for their development and management of operations. Intermediate and minor ports, quite a few of which also handle a significant amount of our foreign trade, are under the control and management of the various maritime state governments. The major ports handle the bulk of our foreign trade and are, therefore, vital gateways for timely shipment of exports and clearance of imports for keeping the production wheels of the economy moving. Nevertheless, their importance is negatively felt when they catch banner headlines of the news media in times of strike and congestion.

Functionally, the major ports have direct berthing facilities and work round the clock and through all weathers. Intermediate and minor ports are generally deficient in these respects as also in terms of handling facilities. Most of them are lighterage ports where night navigation and monsoon operations are difficult. The development of infrastructure and its upgradation are very slow on account of paucity of financial resources plaguing the respective maritime state governments. However, the resource crunch also adversely affects the timely expansion, upgradation and modernisation of facilities at our major ports. Delay in the execution of projects in this regard additionally compound the problem through cost overrun, as has been glaringly demonstrated by the Nhava Shiva port.

In a tradition bound country, port management and operations, by and large, continue to fall into a groove and port practices for the users still tend to be historical. The customs department which is an inextricable part of the port operations has yet to emanicipate itself from the conservatism ill-suited to the needs of growing trade of a fast-moving economy. The port and customs, though these administratively constitute separate agencies, are part of the central government system. They are often at loggerheads which inevitably affect the users interests. In fact, in many instances they are found to be working at cross purposes. Against this background, one naturally looks for an alternative system of managing our ports which will be as efficient as its counterpart in the developed countries.

Generally speaking the system of port administration and management fall into three broad patterns so far as the principal ports in the developed as well as developing conntries are concerned. In most developed countries, especially in

Western Europe and North America, there are "landlord ports" and the so-called "tool ports." In case of the former, the local municipal or similar authority which owns the land strip, lease it out to private agencies to construct and operate the port system.

In the case of the latter, the concerned landowning authority develops the requisite port infrastructure in the form of a berthing system without any handling equipment and other necessary facilities like transit sheds, warehouses and physical movements of cargo, before leasing it out to private agencies.

These agencies are shipping companies, freight forwarders or Stevedoring firms. The management and operations of such ports are, therefore, entrusted to private agencies, prepared to make necessary investment which would obviously vary according to the terms of leasing arrangements. In the third pattern, which largely prevails in the developing countries, the government itself takes upon itself the ownership, development, management and operation of ports. It is generally a matter of policy in India and many other developing countries that the central and the state governments assume direct responsibility in this regard. This is largely on account of the critical needs of the economy, heavy capital investment involved and the strategic nature of port infrastructure. Besides, the developing nature of the economy also demands provision of port services at the least possible cost to the users, without any discrimination.

The port facilities in our country still continue to be very basic in nature supporting the growth of foreign trade and operations of national shipping activities. Therefore, private agencies have so far not been permitted to own and operate these services excepting the professional one of stevedores who are generally engaged by individual shipping companies and customs house agents (clearing and forwarding agents) licensed by customs authorities for clearance of import cargoes and forwarding of export cargoes on behalf of the shippers.

In this increasingly competitive world of international business, the users of port facilities inevitably compare the efficiency and costs prevailing in the developed and developing countries. Once this is done Indian ports do not emerge creditably. As a matter of fact, according to the users, they constitute a virtual disability. The slow process of expansion as well as modernisation of the facilities especially in the context of container technology and handling of large bulk carriers and tankers is particularly noticeable. Besides, port and customs procedurers continue to be clumsy and time-consuming on account of the bureaucratic system.

Under these circumstances, the government, under the pressure of the users' lobby, is toying with idea of privatisation of port facilities with a view to increasing efficiency for the benefit of the users. Recently, Calcutta lort Trust considered for leasing out its container berths at Haldia for management and operation by a private agency. A few foreign shipping companies, reportedly, have shown interest. But with caveats and conditions which may not be acceptable to the port authorities. Similar interest is being shown for the Nhava Shiva port, coming up soon across Bombay, with modern facilities at a considerable cost.

Under the port system existing in the developed countries, the scope for privatisation is inbuilt in the very policy of port development and management. However, India has its own disadvantages. In our prevailing system, when we talk of privatisation, it amounts to creating enclaves or pockets of private operation and management, especially for taking over the container berths. But the major problem seems to be with regard to the employment of labour, investment in handling equipment, fixation of port charges and provision of services without discrimination. Private agencies who could be interested in these matters are the shipping companies especially foreign ones. They would like to take over operation and management of container berths, directly or through their local agents in India, but they would like to come in on their own terms and would insist on a free hand in the employment of requisite personnel and labour. In the prevailing Indian context these would pose problems that are not easy to resolve.

We do not have the system of hire and fire in the employment of personnel. The dock labour boards which usually supply labour for stevedoring operations, cannot be easily kept out if the private agencies want to bring in their own labour for well known reasons. Some degree of preference, if not outright discrimination, is inevitable under private operations in providing services and formulation of charges which would tend to be based on purely commercial considerations. Consequently, one is not sure of the reactions of the users.

However, despite these problems if the private agencies, in coordination with the concerned port authority, can succeed in reversing the general trend of inefficiency, it would be the most welcome development. At the same time one need not give up the hope of upgrading the standard of port operations by suitably gearing its top management, and induction of discipline as well as a spirit of dedication. In this respect the port of Madras provides an encouraging example. Efforts in these directions need to be pursued especially at new ports which have been accorded the status of major in recent times.

2

FRESH DOSE OF PLATITUDES FOR INDIAN SHIPOWNERS

PERSONS occupying high positions in the government as also in the Planning Commission are generally not known for their homework on the subject areas they are supposed to handle with the expected sense of national responsibilities. Our system of government, operational procedures and the inevitably attached weightage of hierarical positions in policy formulations and decision making; discourage motivation or even an inclination to study and understand. There is too much of, on the job learning process going on in a hurried and haphazard manner with ever mounting pressure on time largely consumed by administrative rituals. Therefore, even senisble individuals when given opportunity to use a public forum in the hope of sharing views and understanding the problem of the industry and trade, indulge in platitudes and advice quite redundant and irrelevant to the aituation. It is usually found to be the essiest and safest course. This has exactly happened when the Member, Planning Commission in charge of Transport delivered the Master Memorial Lecture on "Shipping in the Seventh Plan" organised by the Indian Merchant's Chamber in May this year.

While exhorting the Indian shipowners, be laid special emphasis on modernisation rather than expansion, self-help rather than continuing dependence on Government loans, qualitative services and competitive efficiency rather than legislative protection for the industry to take up the challenge. Even conceding that shipping was passing through a difficult period, he observed, "any country anywhere in the world in any areas of manufacturing when they face a problem of this particular type as in shipping, you have got to think not noly of improving the technology level of shipping but also the areas where you have got to more, so that your skill or investments pay much more and much better than wheat is being paid today. . . when changes take place, it does not mean that it is a message of death but it is a challenge to accept the newer modes, now methods of doing things. Recalling the words of late M.A. Master, he reiterated that "answer to the Indian shipping is just not tonnage, it is what type of ship you are going to offer is important."

To quote the fabulous Master without fully knowing and understanding him can be highly misleading. This, columnist who has known him at close quarters can also recall his words when he said, "In the pre-independence years, we had to fight the British Shipowners and British rulers who supported them. Now, in an independent India we have virtually to fight our own government for recognising the status of the shipping industry." He also used to say that Indian shipping was the Cindrella of our industrial household. It has also to be remembered that he fought redentlessly but unsuccessfully for the inclusion of shipping in the core sector of the economy.

The honourable member of the Planning Commission, also advised the shipowners to emulate and follow the examples of Narottam Morarji, Walchand Hirachand and M.A. Master, the pioneers of Indian shipping. This certainly amounted to carry coal to Dhanbad and Jharia if not to New castle. The efforts and the approach of these pioneers for the development of Indian shipping is too wellknown to the existing generation of Indian shipowners whom the honourable member was addressing. As a matter of fact the boot is on the other foot. There is a lot more that the present day policy formulaters have to learn from them. In the fifties and sixties there used to be much more meaningful interaction between the Government and the leaders of the industry on many vital and relevant issues. This became possible because, we had dedicated and knowledgable persons in the government who used to respond sensibly if not always adequately. The very preamble of the historical Merchant Shipping Act of 1958 is a glowing testimony to the collective wisdom of the persons in the Government and the Shipping Industry at that time. It reads as follows:

> "An Act to foster the development and ensure the efficient maintenance of an Indian Mercantile Marine in a manner best suited to serve the nationa interests and for that purpose to establish a National Shipping Board and a Shipping Development Fund, to provide the registeration of Indian ships and generally to amend and consolidate the law relating to merchant shipping."

The Shipping Development Fund Committee constituted under the Act for the administration of the Fund is in the process of being wound up, although it has perpetual succession and a common seal. The Seventh Plan document has suggested a restructuring of the SDFC in view of the chronic condition of global depression which necessitates slavage operation along with restructuring of the industry and technological upgradation. The Plan document also advocates for securing adequate cargo base for ensuring financial viability and acquisition of tonnage to meet the growing requirement of our foreign trade, But the Ministry of Finance appeare to have fallen into the myopic well by totally disregarding the position taken by the Planning Commission. It is accustomed to take a simple accountant's approach in the matter of allocating funds which would always fall short for non-priority or non-core sectors of the economy. Besides, the financial sickness of the shipping industry is uncousciously put on par with that of the shore based industrial units. Therefore, the simplistic logic would be to stop further flow of funds to sick and unproductive units. The bureaucrats in the Finance Ministry would not be able to see the distinction between the domestic and international causes which influence the financial fortunes of the shorebased industry and the shipping industry. The office of the Economic Advisor, in the Ministry of Finance also appears to have failed to play its rote in putting the bureaucrats wise on the subject. Be that as it may. The most relevant question that arises in this context is: Why has the Planning Commission failed in defending the position it has taken on the development of Indian shipping in the Sixth Plan? As a matter of fact, the strategic importance of the industry for trade promotion, foreign exchange earnings and providing logistic support to maintaining essential supplies during civil and military emergencies, particularly in the prevailing international situation should govern the approach of the custodians of national finance. Trade and economic cooperation have now been recognised as important factors in forging friendly ties with other countries on a sustainable basis. At the ground level operation of such a policy one has firt to organise the transport services to carry the trade, aid and exchanges. Even with small island countries like Moratius, Fiji, Laccadives and our own island territories of Andaman Nicobar and Lakwadeep transport services are organised and run at considerable financial lossas. When modern vassels, even of a modest size are employed in such transport linkages, it virtually amounts to asking elephants to carry match boxes. But then these activities have tangible and intangible benefits in subserving larger and long term national interests. The industry which has, therefore to operate for serving a variety of purposes has to be considered quite differently by applying a varied set of parameters. If such basics of the subject are not understood, possibly nothing worthwhile could be understood. If Shri Master were alive today, one shudders to think about his reaction, considering the apathy and ignorance that prevails in the official quarters.

The National Shipping Board has become infructuous. The SDFC is being dismentalled Industrial Credit and Investment Coroporation (ICIC) is reportedly being considered to do a sort of holding operations for the loans advanced by SDFC. The Indian Shipping companies have, therefore, to dend for themselves while they are passing through the worst crisis. A virtual policy vaccum is being developed when Indian shipping is struggling for its very survival.

3

SHADOWS AND SUBSTANCE OF CRISIS IN SHIPPING

A Service industry like shipping, when in crisis, evokes much more interest than during its periods of positive achievements. Besides, in the currently prevailing climate of inverted values, like Gresham's Law—bad coins drive out good coins from circulation—bad news drives out good news from the pages of mass media. In this context, a midweek review of the shipping industry recently brought out by one of the business dailies throws up the views of the leading lights of the industry on the causes of crisis in the shipping industry. The researchers of this daily have also thrown in their own dose of wisdom with the help of some conventional parameters of comparison. All the same, it is a welcome exercise to help generate public awareness on the subject although it may cause only a marginal impact on the process of policy formulation.

There is indisputable consensus on the basic cause of the crisis, *viz.* imbalance between supply of and demand for shipping tonnage or what is popularly termed as overtonnaging. Several factors are resposible for this phenomenon. However, the global situation seems to have improved in terms of the prevailing levels of freight rates, there being upward movements especially in dry cargo and tanker markets. This is attributed to the world tonnage getting into balance with market demand. Obviously, it is based on a certain relationship between the available global shipping tonnage and the total quantity of cargo requiring movement by sea in the international trade. This relationship or the ratio between the two is generally not spelt out by anybody. However, this ratio hovering normally around 1:10 (World shipping tonnage in GRT to originating traffic tonnage in a given year) or any substantial deviation from this has upward or downward impact on the level of the freight rates prevailing in the dry cargo and tanker markets.

A couple of qualifications need be applied to this proposition. Advances in shipbuilding technology have brought in faster and large ships, and mechanized handling of cargo saves port time of the ships. Besides, demand for shipping has to be measured in ton. miles rather than originating cargo tonnage. These factors are usually taken into account in planning, operation and cost of voyages with regard to specific movements between the ports of loading and discharge and with reference to specific commodities as well as the volumes to be moved. But, in the context of the global scale, several variable and uncertain factors do invariably intervene to upset the calculations with heavy distortions on account of trading, commercial, political, financial and labour factors, which help keep the movements of international trade in a state of perpetual flex. Technological means, which have helped us in reducing the distance and the time barriers, are often neutralized by these factors. Inevitably, therefore, how much the ratio of 1:10 may have changed on a global scale, is very difficult to assess,

The liner shipping sector involved in the movement of general cargo is far more complex. Traditionally, it has been characterized by administered freight rates through the institution of the conference system or Freight Agreement Association established historically on numerous trade routes of the World. It is a segment of international shipping that is traditionally insulated from the normal interaction of the forces of supply and demand. Prices on freight rates are kept relatively stable for short and medium-term periods through a common tariff of rates among the member lines.

However, upward general revisions of tariff rates across the board are periodically effected on account the worldwide phenomenon of escalation in costs due to inflationary forces. During the current recession, these rates also got subjected to market forces on account of overtonnaging and weakening of the conference system. With emergence of cut-throat competition, line rates on certain routes got so much depressed that they barely covered the fuel cost of the services provided to the shippers. Besides, in liner shipping, freight rates usually cover the cost of loading, discharge, stowage and handling of cargo over and above the usual cost of transportation service. Liner shipping companies are, therefore, passing through a double squeeze, *viz.* uneconomic level of freight rates and escalation in the cargo handling costs, especially in India, and at the ports of most developing countries. Therefore, any improvement in the charter freight markets for dry bulk or liquid bulk cargoes has hardly any direct relationship with and impact on the fortunes of liner shipping. Whatever improvement takes place in the freight revenue earning is dependent on the organizational strength of the institutional conference system on diffe-rent trade routes of the world *vis-a-vis* the strength of independent operators. In this context, the emergence of the Minimum Freight Agreement (MFA), which virtually brings the outsiders within the fold of the conference system, will help raise the level of the liner freight rates.

Inevitably, therefore, when we dilate upon the causes and remedies of crisis in global shipping, the basic difference between the tramp and liner segments of commercial shipping activities and their nature of operations has to be fully recognized. The shipowners who have operated or are, by and large, operating in the dry bulk carriers and tanker markets, willy-nilly, are prone to bring in the problems of dealing with the market forces in the forms of bulks and bears operating all the time. The volatile nature of these markets would necessitate maximum freedom and flexibility in not only operating and managing the ships but also in purchasing and selling as well as chartering in and chartering out of vessels. At the same time, they need assurance for participation in the movement of bulk cargoes purchased and sold on government account, in order to minimize the exposure to business hazards in times of prolonged depression in the charter markets. The patronage to domestic shipbuilding yards is also not favoured on account of high costs and prolonged delivery schedules.

The liner shipowners' biggest bugbear is the cut-throat competition, which was largely kept at bay or at least in manageable proportions for a good part of this century through a stable and viable conference system. As a matter of fact, liner shipping was made more secure and viable through bilateral shipping arrangements between many developing and socialist countries. Therefore, one has to necessarily examine the causes of the crisis in both the tramping and liner sectors of the industry rather than separately on account of their structural and operational differences.

However, the phenomenon of overtonnaging and the advances in shipping technology have an impact on both the sectors, but it has manifested itself quite differently in qualitative and quantitative terms. Evidently, when a set of very general questions is addressed to two categories of Indian shipowners—one operating in the market-oriented charter markets and the other operating in liner shipping and only one representing a composite shipping company like the SCI—it is difficult to get enlightening answers.

In a mixed economy like ours, it is pointless to ask for or advocate complete freedom of operations. The recent experiences of free markets in countries like the USA have shown disastrous results. Whether it is a shore-based industry or shipping, a policy-mix of regulatory and support measures with a fair degree of freedom within the broad policy parameters, appears to be the most pragmatic and sensible way out of the crisis. However, it is pretty clear that without a meaningful and effective consensus on the desired policy mix among the Indian shipowers in the private as well as the public sectors, it would be very difficult, under the present dispensation, to secure the requisite measures expeditiously.

The key factor for the development and sustenance of the Indian mercantile marine is the effective development of tonnage and generation of adequate freight revenue. This would, logically, require a stable cargo base, without which no plans for expansion and modernization of our fleet ean be meaningful or feasible.

In contrast to the global scenario, the cargo generated in India's foreign trade has shown a steady trend although the level of freight revenue has gone down on account of the recession in the freight market and cut-throat competition in the liner trades. The policy of *laissez faire* in keeping the Indian trade totally free and open does not make any sense in the prevailing climate of cut-throat competition. Even the operations of stock exchanges and commodity markets, which predominantly operate on the basis of market forces, are subjected to control and regulatory measures when the situation degenerates into manipulation of the market through unfair means. If the Indian shipping industry and its users are not able to devise ways and means for promoting a viable and sustainable relationship, the official machinery has no option but to step in to stem the rot. We can illaffard a policy of drift or indecision in a segment of our economy, which has to encounter the challenge of growing trade deficits.

4

STRENGTHENING THE OPERATIONAL BASE FOR INDIAN SHIPPING

THERE is no disputing the fact that export promotion has become a critical and crucial policy plank of the Government of India, so all obstacles in promoting the sale of Indian goods abroad have to be removed forthwith. The Market Development Assistance Fund at the disposal of the Ministry of Commerce has now crossed Rs. 1,000 crores as per the current budgetary provisions. Besides, the liberalized import policy with substantial reductions in import duties on capital goods and industrial raw materials, exemption of profits on export transactions from income-tax and a host of direct and indirect props for promoting exports already in existence for a decade-and-a-half should gladden the hearts of out hard-boiled businessmen. It has also not to be forgotten that quite a sizeable proportion of our exports benefits from the undeclared devaluation (or call it a depreciation of the rupee) under the present system of adjustment in its value against the so-called basket of currencies. Therefore, if exports from the country have to be generated at any cost for reducing the balance-of-payments deficits, on what logic can we ignore the loss of foreign exchange incurred by allowing foreign vessels to carry a disproportionate share of highfreighted general cargo in our export trade ?

Like the USSR, India had realized long back the need for earning the much needed free foreign exchange by operating a part of its fleet in the cross trades even at a loss. The USA, having realized the importance of trade in services, has succeeded in bringing the subject on the agenda of the GATT to strengthen its share eventually at the cost of the developing countries in Asia, Africa and Latin America, which too have resorted to measures for maintaining a viable cargo base for operation of their mercantile marine, as also for conserving and earning the much needed foreign exchange. In contrast, we in this country seem to be myopic, buttressing the position taken by the Indian shippers, who are out for short-term gains. This is positively irrational at the level of national policy and any Ministry or Department of the Government of India, which persists in upholding only a sectoral view, is not serving the realization of the accepted objectives of the Government Policy. The consequences of such a state of affairs are clearly before us.

The shipping fleet of the country has gone down from a peak of over 6.3 million GRT as on January 1985 to 5.6 million GRT in January 1988. This has happened despite the fact that our external trade reached a peak of over 133 million tons in terms of traffic handled by our major ports in 1987-88. It also needs to be emphasized that out of the present level of our shipping tonnage, a sizable proportion is laid up, being not actively in operation. This includes the Scindia's fleet of 22 ships and the ships of a few other companies, which are now defunct.

The liner sector of our shipping fleet is in a pathetic state for want of cargo suppot. The drain of foreign exchange is here maximum, because it consists of relatively high-freighted cargo. This has also left a great adverse financial impact on Indian lines operating liner services. The great Scindia Company has folded up. The India Steam is just managing to keep its head above water. The Shipping Corporation of India (SCI), which is now the only major operator in the liner trades, is incurring huge losses in that sector, and is able to show some overall profit on account of its operations in the bulk sector, especially in carriage of crude oil and petroleum products. Its position in the liner trades could be improved only by acquisition of container ships for providing efficient services on matching basis with those provided by foreign flags. But it appears that its plans in this regard could not materialize for want of timely approval by the Public Investment Board and the requisite sanctions from the Ministry of Finance. Perhaps the SCI management lost much of the enthusiasm in this regard for want of cargo support measures being promised and pronounced by the Ministry of Surface Transport but without any implemental action over the last six years. After all, modern cellular ships involve heavy investment with enhanced risk particularly in the apathetic and hostile climate prevailing against Indian shipowners, especially the SCI. It is a pity that when the freight market is showing some visible signs of improvement, the SCI has been virtually obliged to terminate the charters of the container ships employed in the UK-Continent and US trades on account of escalations in the charter rates. Consequently, it is now obliged to use its own combi ships, which cannot match, in providing service, full-fledged container ships. Once again SCI and other Indian shipping companies would miss the opportunity of taking advantage of the improved conditions of the freight market, because the planned acquisition of modern container ships is not timely enough.

No developing maritime country can afford to repeat such tragic situations too often. Private sector shipping companies are already shying away from the liner operations. Even SCI as a public sector company has been obliged to withdraw from the West Asia, Gulf and West African trades on account of the losses suffered for want of cargo support. On the routes now being operated with combi ships, the losses in the liner sector would continue to mount. With the usual conceptual confusion on liner shipping and wholly unreasonable expectations of a public sector shipping company, there is every possbility of the persons in high authority arriving at wrong conclusions and possibly unwise decisions thereof. This would open up floodgates for massive intrusion of foreign flags and Indian shipping would be obliged to commit *harakiri*.

In this woefully dismal picture, some silver linings are still discernible. *Firstly*, the shipping companies operating in the liner trades all over the globe have been forced to accept the conventional wisdom that they can survive only on a collective basis. Operating separately, they would easily hang themselves, one by one, through cut-throat competition. This is clearly indicated by the emergence of Minimum Freight Agreements (MFA) or Minimum Rate Agreements (MRA) in the Indian trades and similar understanding in other trades. Inevitably, this development is going to catch up and stability of rates on the basis of financially viable liner services will have to be established for serving the needs of the trade in general cargoes. The shippers in their own interest should realize the advantage of this, instead of hankering after short-term and arbitary financial gains arising from the cut-throat competition and chaotic conditions of liner services.

Another favourable signal is the realization, albeit belated, on the part of the Ministry of Finance, of the gravity of the situation created by financial collapse of the established shipping companies in the private sector, involving loss of sizable government funds advanced as loan finance. But, the most intractable position is with regard to a public sector company like the SCI. If it continues to incur losses in the liner trades, there would not only be a constant drain on the resources of the Government but also a sizable loss of foreign exchange. At the same time, the presence of a strong Indian shipping company in the liner trades with a significant share is very much needed in the overall national interest. This has been proved on a number of occasions in the past. It has become all the more necessary in the context of the larger alliance of foreign lines being forged in the wake of the Minimum Freight Agreement being established on the major trade routes of the country. If this is not realized fully, foreign interests would easily overwhelm the

Indian trade, rendering even the Government of India helpless in the matter. It is hoped that the gravity of the situation is fully recognized by Government, particularly by the Ministry of Finance, which, above all, would be in a position to bring round the recalcitrant elements in other user Ministries doting on ihe government finance.

5

COMPLEX KALEIDOSCOPE OF PORT OPERATIONS

INDIAN ports are literally as well as figuratively always at the receiving end. They receive the cargoes from the carriers or the shippers, keep them in custody till cleared and forwarded by the owners or their agents, of course after having received the blessings or brickbats from the customs authorities. The entry and exit of cargoes are rigidly regulated physically as well technically in conformity with port byelaws, Customs Act and the regime of duties and dues applicable to different categories of imports and exports. In this process, pulls and counter-pulls are always operating on the movement of cargoes, resulting in a perpetual conflict between the objectives of conformity to values and financial accountability. However, efficient functioning of our port system is very crucial to foreign trade operations and the developmental needs of the national economy But then, it has to be recognized that overall efficiency is dependent upon the coordinated co-generating of a multiplicity of official and non-official agencies involved in the complex kaleidoscope of port operations. Mere provision of adequate and modern infrastructure facilities for berthing of ships, handling of cargoes and warehousing, although basic to the needs of the port users, is not enough for efficient functioning of our ports. Any component can assume the role of the spider in the web and can influence the overall operations favourably or unfavourably. In the light of these basics, one has to react to the comments and suggestions made by the Parliamentary Committees from time to time. The latest one in this regard is the 43rd Report of the Estimates Committee (1986-87), presented to the Lok Sabha in April 1987. A major obsession of these committees at present and in the immediate past has been the establishment of the Central Ports Authority, which is expected to resolve our port problems by promoting coordination in operations, planning and development of major ports. The matter was examined in depth by the Major Ports Reforms Committee comprising past and present Chairmen of the major ports, independent experts and representatives of the customs, labour and various official and non-official agencies. After long deliberations, the Committee reached the conclusion that setting up of such a National Ports Authority is not feasible and useful to serve the intended purpose. The apparent advantage a unified set-up is liable to offer would be more than offset by the problems it will throw up, the principal among these bring intergration of the personnel of all major ports. The assumption that a unified authority will strengthen the managment and help the units become economically viable is somewhat far-fetched. Generally, the larger the organization, the more difficult it is to manage. Even if this does not turn out to be so in the instant case and the proposed authority is set up and the administrative Ministry given continued and final say on major and minor issues of policy as of now, the Authority's major preoccupation would really descend to the level of monitoring and overseeing day-to-day fuctioning of the ports. The unified Authority with all the organizational apparatus will, in effect, thus only become yet another tier between the Government and the ports. The MPRC strongly felt that even in the existing setting, without a middle tier in between, the relationship between the ports and the administrative Ministry can be made more business-like. With a view to achieving this, the MPRC has recommended the setting up of Major Ports Development Board in the Ministry with the Secretary, Ministry of Surface Transport, as Chairman; Additional Secretary (Ports) as Vice Chairman; and Financial

Advisor in the Ministry, representatives of the Ministries of Finance, Commerce and Railways, the Chairmen of major ports and two eminent outside profes sionals as members. The Board will be responsible for:

(a) Overall planning and intergrated development of all major ports;

(b) Investment decisions;

(c) Securing optimal utilization of manpower and other assets;

(d) Coordination with the Planning Commission and other Governmental agencies;

(e) Management of the Port Development Fund (recommended by the MPRC); and

(f) Evaluation/appraisal of all port project.

The Estimates Committee does not subscribe to the view that the creation of a single statutory body will in any way create "yet another tier" between the Government and the ports. The Committee stresses that its concept of a Central Ports Authority is a single apex body not only to evolve port policies on a common, uniform and expert basis, but also to administer, coordinate and monitor all the activities and operations of major ports, in lieu of the existing multiplicity of administrative bodies of the prots like National Shipping Board, National Harbour Board, Conference of Chairmen of Major Ports and, last but not least, the systematically swelling Indian Ports Association. According to the Estimates Committee, the establiment of the Major Ports Development Board, recommended by the MPRC, not only falls woefully short of the scope and function envisaged for the Central/National Ports Authority but creates also yet another administrative body to monitor the development activities of the Ports in addition to the existing multiple authorities. The Estimates Committee has, therefore, finally stressed the need for the establishment of the National Ports Authority, so that overall administration, planning and development of major ports could be run on sound commercial lines and not like attached autonomous offices of the Government as they appear to be functioning at present.

There appears to be a lot of confusion in understanding the type of administrative set-up operating for planning and development of our major ports. Besides, the system of administration and management of our ports also does not seem to have been adequately understood. As a matter of fact, the two aspects have got mixed up in the thinking of the Estimates Committee. Moreover, the multiple bodies, referred to by the Estimates Committee, have been set up for different objectives in view. The National Shipping Board does not exclusively deal with port matters, It was created for advising the Government on the various facets of the National Shipping Policy. Although the National Harbour Board deals exclusively with port matter, its role is more of an advisory character, based on the feedback received from various user-interests. The Conference of Chairmen of Major Ports is more for interaction and experience-sharing required for dealings with the problems of port management. The functions of the Indian Ports Association are clear enough and cannot be confused with the actual functioning of ports and management of port operations. Therefore, the wave lengths of the Estimates Committee and MPRC on the question of creating a Central Ports Authority are different. However, as per the newspaper reports, the Government has now decided to establish the National Ports Authority, obviously under the pressure of the Parliamentry Committee. One can only wish well to this venture but its emergence would be full of apprehensions on the part of the providers and users of port services.

6

MOTHER-IN-LAW SYNDROME BACK IN INTERNATIONAL SHIPPING

THE REVIEW of the UN Code of Conduct for Liner Conferences is slated for discussion at the forum of UNCTAD. There has been literally a "sea-change" in the global scenario of shipping since the adoption of the Code. It would be in order to refresh our memory about the Code, so that its relevance is not lost in understanding the new scenario that has emerged. International shipping had witnessed the most prolonged period of recession in its recorded history. This was brought about by an unprecedented supply/ demand imbalance in the wake of decline in global trade movements and massive expansion of tonnage propelled by modern technology of scales. The advances in ship-building technology gave rise to the emergence of giant tankers, large bulk carriers and sophisticated container ships in the liner trades. Consequently, the capital-intensive nature of the industry got accentuated many more times than the hitherto prevailing level a decade-and-a-half back. This put the developing maritime countries with scarce capital resources at a great disadvantage. It is not easy for them to jump on the band-wagon of advanced technology at once through obsolescence of the existing fleet except in a phased manner despite the unbearable pressures and compulsions from the competitive situation generated by the shipowners and shippers from the developed market countries.

As it is, the participation of the developing countries in the carriage of the global trade is quite low on account of lower ownership share of the world merchant fleet. This is now computed around 20 per cent —132.3 million DWT. Their share of the tankers fleet is only 16.4 per cent, and of the bulk carriers fleet 24.8 per cent. In the high freighted segment of general cargo trades catered to by liner tonnage the share is around 26.5 per cent and is the lowest at 12 per cent in the containership fleet of the world. Even the spread of this meagre shipping tonnage, about 60 per cent, is concentrated in only seven developing countries, namely Brazil, India, Iran, Philippines, South Korea, Singapore and Hong Kong. A large number of other developing countries are, therefore, virtually dependent on the carriers of developed countries for the carriage of their overseas trades. Even countries like India and Brazil, which have struggled hard to develop the fleet, have found it increasingly difficult to sustain operational and financial viability in the face of cut-throat competition emerging from the phenomenon of overtonnaging, largely brought about by the developed maritime countries and speculative operators attracted by the technology boom.

The long drawn out recession in shipping depressed the freight in the tanker and bulk carrier markets. This virtually disabled, if not totally dismantled, the institution of the Conference System in the liner trades. With the emergence of independent liner operators, the liner freight rates were rendered negotiable and subjected to bargaining to an extent and a scale never witnessed before. Under the circumstances the nascent fleets of developing countries have been pushed to the wall. Once again they have to fight for their survival. Against this backdrop, one has to examine the change in the attitude of the developed maritime countries (DMCs) on the eve of the review of the Liner Code, which was adopted much against their overt and covert opposition.

It must be stated quite frankly that the DMCs did not like to give up their control over the global fleet in the past—more so, now. And they are reviving the old thesis of leaving the field open to those, who have the capability of providing shipping services in the most efficient manner to serve the global trade. In the process, they may as well consider the Liner Code to have become historical, particularly in the light of the altered scenario. The two-track negotiations, one on commodities and the other on services, under the auspices of the GATT are ominously looming large and the developed countries appear hard put to defend their legitimate right to develop the mercantile marine of their own.

Once again, the developing countries have to justify their case for owning and expanding their national fleets without getting overwhelmed by the very familiar argument of better capability with superior technology deployed by the DMCs in serving the international trade. Basically, the principal grounds of justification could be as follows:

(a) The development of the mercantile marine has to be viewed in the integrated context of overall economic development of the developing countries.

(b) The economic development of the newly industrialized countries inevitably requires imported inputs of a much larger magnitude. This would require in turn considerable growth in exports, adequate enough to pay for the growing import bill of individual countries.

(c) It would mean a quantum jump in the growth of exports, which could be realized by continuing growth in exports of traditional items to traditional destinations as also through the strategy of diversification in terms of products and destinations. A host of non-traditional items, especially value-added manufactures and semi-processed items, have to be promoted to destinations in traditional and non-traditional/new markets.

(d) Logically, such an export trade strategy would require promotional shipping services, which have necessarily to be run at considerable losses in initial years till adequate traffic develops to ensure their commercial and financial viability. As seen in the past, such a task could be entrusted only to national shipping lines, because foreign flags would not be willing to undertake such services at a loss *ab initio*. As a matter of fact, there have been cases, where foreign lines have intruded into the trade routes after the national lines, through their efforts and financial sacrifices, developed adequate flows of traffic.

(e) Considering the fair-weather-friend attitude of foreign lines, they cannot be relied upon for serving the trade in times of crisis on accont of civil or military strife. The developing countries have, therefore, to maintain in their own interest fleets of their own as a measure of self-reliance.

(f) Quite often, the trade and shipping interests of a country operate in a tandem to score advantage in the highly competitive international trading operations against countries with weak and comparatively less efficient fleets. The latter would need time and cargo support to be on par with the former. Besides, diversification of trade would require a composite fleet with specialized carriers. Any lacuna in this regard would enhance their dependence on others, who would tend to exploit the situation in their favour.

(g) Trade follows the flag is an old adage. It represents a fundamental truism and its modern version could be that trade cannot flow without logistic support of transport services. The two operations have an automatic integration and have to complement each other. This vital nexus could prove highly vulnerable in the absence of a dependable national mercantile marine.

(h) For developing countries, earning and saving foreign exchange resources by a rational use of the available national fleets is of crucial importance. The developed countries should not grudge this on any count, because there would be enough scope for operation of their fleets without being over-ambitious.

The recent experience has graphically demonstrated that left to themselves, developed countries are prone to first indulge in overtonnaging and then resort to wasteful competition in an obvious attempt to restore the supply/demand balance. This has given rise to Waste of enormous resources. The technology race of going in for the first, second, third and fourth generation containerships has brought ruin to the US shipping line and many others, who suffered from competition. It is time to consider a global mechanism through some international understanding to maintain the supply/demand balance in shipping. The hazards of the shipping business should be minimized by keeping out speculative forces and fly-by-night operators, aided and abetted by the opportunities provided by FOC or open registry countries.

Developed countries, which generally keep on emphasizing the benefits of a free international trading system on a multilateral pattern, do not hesitate to pursue protectionist policies as and when their national interests so demand. The recent US Trade Act and the various restrictive measures adopted with regard to the otherwise free access to the US market are examples in point. As for trade in services, the refrain is once again free access to markets in developed as well as developing countries. The advocacy of freedom of trade without any restrictions in the form of cargo preference or reservation in favour of national bottoms comes into vogue, when developed countries enjoy a bargaining advantage on the basis of commercial and economic strength acquired througe advanced technology. Therefore the positions, generally taken on international trade in merchandise and in services like commercial shipping arse at variance. The maxim of convenience seems to be at work. This may work as a short-term policy, but it is bound to boomerang over a period of time and would hurt the interests of developing countries and damage the global trading system. Under the circumstances, developing countries should once again take a united and collective stand on these matters in UNCTAD and GATT by rejuvenating the spirit of the late 'sixties and early ,seventies. It is necessary to realize that the present international transportation system, based on sophisticated technology, influences the flow of trade to the advantage of the developed countries.

7

PERFUNCTORY ROLE OF NATIONAL SHIPPING BOARD

THE NATIONAL Shipping Board enjoys the status of the highest policy advisory body in terms of the statutory provisions of the Merchant Shipping Act, 1958. However, in reality its functioning has become perfunctory and reporting ritualistic. It is easy to catch on one of the many problems, the shipping industry has been facing but it requires considerable effort and expertise to formulate recommendations and measures for implemental action by the Government machinery. The Ministry of Surface Transport constitutes one of the many cogs in the sprawling and unwieldy adminstrative Government machine. Under the present dispensation, unless that cog acquires critical importance and receives the importance it deserves, the problems of the industry would keep on recyclying from time to time and the requisite measures would remain in perpetual abeyance.

It was, therefore, precisely for the purpose of injecting a sense of urgency for galvanising the government machine to the task in initiating timely measures to resolve the problems of the industry that a statutory Board was constituted. Unfortunately, it has not lived upto the expectations, especially in the time of crisis.

At the first meeting of the present Board held in March 1986, the Minister of State for Surface Transport referred to the continuing recession in shipping. He stated that while the Government of India was seriously engaged in finding ways and means to help the industry to overcome the present crisis, the Board would also assist the effort of the Government by engaging itself in tendering useful advice on some of the important aspects like present condition of shipping companies and shipyards, prevailing level of freight rates, share of Indian ships in India's foreign trade, sophistication in the methods of carriage and need for specialised vessels for various products. He further emphasised the urgent need for the Board to list out the priorities for in-depth deliberations and formulating necessary recommendations for overcoming the existing probles of the industry for consideration of the Government.

He also maintained that achievement of tonnage targets fixed should not be the only index of growth of shipping and that there should be further improvement in the age composition of the total fleet introduction of specialised carriers and cellular vessels. He stressed the need for development of coastal shipping in an integrated fashion with rail and road transportation, keeping in view the economies of the sea transportation. He drew attention as the Board to maritime fraud and suggested that this should be identified and efforts made to eliminate it.

During its two years tenure, the Board held five meetings for deliberations. It constituted two sub-committees, one for reviewing the licensing policy for national bottoms and the other for study of the problems of sailing vessels at the Bombay harbour. It also recommended, in August 1986, that the Government should constitute an expert body consisting of representatives of concerned Ministries and those concerned with the shipping industry for exploring suitable remedialm easures for implemental action by the Government.

The Ministry has since constituted a high level Inter-Ministerial Committee under the Chairmanship of the Director

General of Shipping for a regular dialogue with the members of the shipping fraternity. Besides, the chairman, the committee consists of Joint Secretaries from the Ministry of Surface Transport incharge of shipping and ports. Ministry of Commerce in charge of infrastructure, Ministry of Finance in charge of Banking and a representative of Shipping Credit and Investment Corporation of India (SCICI).

The Board recommended to the Ministry the expeditious clearance of acquisition proposals submitted by various shipping companies in the public and private sectors and urged the concerned authorities in the Government to take speedy decisions in the matter of clearance of sale and purchage of ships.

However, pursuant to the abolition of SDFC, a new committee known as the Ship Acquisition Licensing Committee (SALC) has started functioning since April 1987 to consider applications for acquisition of ships. Financial assistance to private sector shipping companies is now being decided by the Banking Division/SCICI on the basis of financial viability studies. The Empowered Committee of the Banking Division has already taken a decision in-principle to permit shipping companies to diversify into other lines of business so as to withstand the stress and strain of recessionary times, Financial assistance to the public sector shipping company. SCI, will continue to be provided by the Ministry of Surface Transport.

However, some of the observations made by the Chairman of the NSB and quite a few recommendations made by the Board are intriguing as well as interesting. Let me first take up the Chairman's observations which deserve comment.

"Over the years, the Shipping Corporation of India has grown in size. Consequently, this organisation in terms of both men and materials has grown immensely and of control has vastly widened, Government may consider whether it would be a sound commerial decision to develop another shipping company in the public sector."

The present size of SCI is on account of historical and operational factors as well as overall national considerations. When the Eastern India Shipping Corporation and Western Indian Shipping Corporation could not operate as viable units, they were merged 1962 and SCI was formed with the merger of the two corporations. When the Jayanti Shipping Company developed financial and management troubles its fleet was handed over to SCI for operation and maintaining the growth of the Indian fleet. More recently, the Mogul Lines had to be merged with SCI on account of the mounting losses in its operations.

In the process, SCI has grown into a large composite company combining within itself world-wide liner as well as tramping services. Besides as a public sector enterprise it has necessarily to involve itself in lhe coastal and adjacent trades and is under virtual obligation to provide services to Andaman and Nicobar as well as Lakshadweep Islands at the behest of the Home ministry for strategic and developmental reasons. In the past to subserve the diversification strategy of Indian export products it had to initiate several promotional services at considerable loss under pressure of the Ministry of Commerce. Passenger services to South East Asia and East Africa to serve the ethnic population of Indian origin and the Haj services for facilitating pilgrimage of Indian muslims to Mecca were maintained and some of them are still being operated on non-commercial basis. Even the service to Mauritius has been recently started at the behest of the Ministry of External Affairs for strengthening trade and economic co-operation with that Island country occupying a strategic position in the Indian Ocean.

It also needs to be mentioned that in the present context the Government of India is the largest exporter and importer by virtue of its increasing role in the developmental, commercial and trading activities through its various agencies and numerous public sector corporations. The involvement of SCI as a public sector corporation is sizable. Quite often it has to act as the carrier of ultimate resort when neither the foreign nor Indian carriers are available or unwilling to offer their services.

In order to meet such a heavy demand on its services on account of all these factors, it had necessarily to expand its fleet commeunsurate with the growth and composition of India's foreign trade. Inevitably, its organisational structure has become large for managing the largest fleet of ships owned by an Indian company. However, it is not an unusual phenomenon. There are shipping companies in the world which are far bigger than SCI. Mitsui OSK Line (MOL), the Japanese company owns, a fleet of 284 ships of over 11 million DWT. SCI, at present has a fleet of 130 ships with over 4.7 million DWT. (This includes 10 offshore supply vessels also). This is not even half of the fleet operated by MOL.

Besides, with the growing intensity of capital investment in ships and extended nature of shipping operation, the larger companies are in a better position to realise operational and commercial viability. This also explains the rationale behind formation of consortia of shipping companies in recent times. However, it does not mean that any changes in the organisation and management systems are precluded. Under the circumstances, the observation of the Board's Chairman made without any in-depth study of this aspect appears to be facile.

It should be mentioned here that a comprehensive study on SCI has already been done by the office the Comptroller and Auditor General of India and submitted during the last session of the Parliament. Its findings would throw better guidelines for the Government if any structural changes are warranted for improving the performance of the Corporation.

He also observes that development of inadequate infrastructure at our ports is very important for the development of Indian shipping. "In the context of growing containerisation throughout the world, I have no doubt that be must develop our port facilities to handle containers at all major ports, even in the face of financial stringency." It seems that there exists a report of the Major Ports' Reform Committee with an in-depth study on the subject. It is either not known or ignored. Considering the nature of the container technology and the amount of organisational problems faced in the induction of this technology nobody in his wisdom can come forward with such a blanket suggestion.

On the important question of cargo support to national ships, the Board has urged the Government to expedite the implementation of the UN Convention on the Code of Conduct for liner conferences which India has already ratified, by enacting a legislation to implement its relevant provisions. Much water has flown down the Ganges, since the Government initiated its efforts in this regard. It is very evident that the Board does not seem to have grasped or bothered to study as to why the Government has failed to meet with any success in implementing the provisions of the Code. It would have been worthwhile for the Board to identify the forces responsible for stalling the efforts of the Government in this regard and strengthen its will to act decisively through appropriate administrative measures to frustrate the attempts of regressive forces who want to perpetuate the nefarious status quo, and expose the system to further deterioration.

Equally facile is the reference about the lack of container ships in the Indian fleet. The chairman states "...while rest of the world is moving rigidly towards containerisation, our container fleet is almost negligible." Immediately the next sentence which follows states, "Moreover, Indian shipping suffers from inadequate infrastructure support facilities...". This virtually amounts to begging the question. In the absence of any cargo measures, with poor port infrastructure, lack of financial resources and with cut-throat competition prevailing in liner shipping, can the Board present any magic wand to Indian shipowners with the help of which it can not only present themselves with containerships but also operate them on a commercially viable basis!

The NSB does not really function as an expert advisory body. It has become a loose conglomerate of various interests and partisan groups. In the very nature of things such an entity is not in a position to produce a meaningful report to serve any useful purpose. For reasons best known to itself the Board has also denied itself any assistance of professionals who know the intricacies of various facets of the industry. Consequently, the report not only lacks the substance but also a coherence in presentation.

8

SHIPPERS' STANCE PUTS GOVERNMENT IN THE DOCK

IT APPEARS legitimate for shippers' organisation to pick on every possible cause on behalf of its members and agitate against the shipping lines without looking backward or forward. Unfortunately, it has almost become a tradition in their relationship on the West Coast of India. Currently, the bone of contention hangs round the increase in freight rates by the Karmahom conference and the hike in the recovery of pershipment expenses involved in the Terminal Handling Charges for containers (THC) at the port of Bombay by the shipping lines. Prima facie, these issues directly escalate and add to the landed cost of our export shipments to West European destinations and provide a legitimate base for Indian shippers to agitate. However, the important question is against whom they should agitate. They appear to do so against the shipping lines more out of force of habit, without going into the basics of the matter.

In liner shipping for break-bulk cargoes, it is customary for the carrier to assume the responsibility for loading, stowage and discharge of cargo on behalf of the shippers on cost recovery basis. But the expenses incurred thereon are integrated with the freight charged for providing the transportation service. The former is neither shown nor collected separately and, therefore, becomes an inbuilt part of the tariff rates. In other words, the carrier accepts the cargo on full liner terms. Only in the services provided under the bilateral shipping agreements, for example, in the India-USSR trade that the tariff rates are on the FIO (Free In and Out) basis and the carrier while assuming the responsibility for loading stowage and discharge would charge separately for the expenses involved.

With the emergence of container technology, the pre-shipment cost and incidental expenses involved prior to loading the containers on board the vessel are calculated and charged separately by the carrier, over and above the freight charge for providing the transportation services in our export trades. Broadly an inventory of various items of preshipment cost at the port of Bombay would be as follows:

1. Transportation of empty container to stuffing point;
2. Lift on, of empty container at the depot;
3. Empty container lift of BPT (TLT) at stuffiing point;
4. Stuffing cost payable to stevedores on the basis of box rate as per Bombay Stevedores Association's tariff;
5. Stuffing cost payable to port;
6. Gate/shed night allowance;
7. Customs appraiser/examination;
8. Fork lift and other miscellaneous;
9. Lift on, of loaded container at stuffing point;
10. Transportation of container to the vessel including lift off/lift on at prestack and drayage to hook point;
11. Gate/shed opening charges in the docks;
12. Container wharfage/ground rent payable to BPT; and
13. Receiving cargo in shed.

It needs to be stated here that the above items represent all possible items of expenses, and are not necesarily applicable as preshipment expenses in all cases. However, items like stuffing cost, transportation to vessel and multiple lift on and lift off of the containers, represent a major proportion of the total preshipment expenses involved at the port of Bombay. These will have to be incurred in the case of all export shipments containerised at designated centres by the BPT. No doubt these expenses work out very much on the high side on account of lack of adequate space in the port area, improvised handling facilities for the cargo as well as containers and extra loading of labour cost which the container technology is expected to reduce drastically. They adversely affect the shippers as well as shipowners. Under normal circumstances, shipowners should be able to recover them fully from the shippers since these expenses are incurred on their behalf purely on recovery basis.

However, under a situation of pay much lower, about 15 per cent only than what ought to have refrained from full recovery and shippers have got accustomed to pay much lower, about 15 per cent only than what ought have been levied as preshipment cost. It is also well recognised that shippers cannot pay more. Likewise, in a period of acute recession the shipping lines also cannot afford to subsidise these expenses. We are, therefore, in a catch-22 situation which can be resolved only by apportioning the burden on concerned interests *viz.*, shippers, shipowners, port authorities and labour, till the overall situation gets rationalised through various long-term measures.

In this context, it needs to be reiterated that in the high cost economy of ours, increase in labour productivity has assumed paramount importance. It has become not only important but critical at our ports. The strength of the labour gangs employed, especially at Bombay port needs to be rationalised and all kinds of work stoppages have to be discouraged.

Obviously this is a matter, in which, neither the shippers nor the shipowners are in a position to do anything tangible. It rests squarely with the port authorities and concerned ministries of the Government. By raking up this issue, surely, the shippers have literally put the Government in the dock.

The complaint lodged by the Western India Shippers' Association (WISA) with the Monopolies and Restrictive Trade Practices Commission (MRTPC) against Karmahom Conference for alleged violation of the UN Code for liner conferences and formation of illegal monopolistic cartel through Minimum Freight Agreement (MFA) among the conference and non-conference lines, has given rise to an interesting situation.

A similar reference, although in a different context, was made to MRTPC in 1976 without any tangible outcome. As a matter of fact the MRTPC could not make any headway on the complaint for want of any written evidence from the shippers. However, this time hopefully, the shippers organisation would not allow it to happen again. But the moot point is whether MRTPC has any rightful jurisdiction over international shipping conferences with multinational membership. Basically, it is a commission meant to deal with the monopoly and restrictive practices in the domestic trade.

Shippers organisation seems to be inspired by the example of Federal Maritime Commission (EMC), a statutory agency set up under the provision of the US Shipping Act of 1916 which was enacted on the basis of the findings of the Alexander Committee, Indian shippers and their spokesmen should not forget that in the free market oriented economy of USA the existence of monopolies and cartels were outlawed under the Sherman anti-trust laws, and therefore, the very existence of the conference system came to be questioned. The Department of Judiciary wanted totally ban the shipping conference in the US commerce whereas the Department of Commerce thought otherwise. The latter realised the utility of its institutionalised services in the liner trades in the absence of any other viable alternative. It was apprehended that if the shipping conferences which had become universal by then were disbanded under anti-trust laws, the US commerce would get isolated and the country would have to face the inevitable consequences. Therefore, ultimately, they had to be given the requisite status by confering immunity from the provision of the anti-trust legislation.

However, FMC was setup to exercise surveillance on the activities of the conferences which could acquire potent and latent powers to exploit and discriminate the users of their services. It has also to be noted that shippers organisations were also not permitted under the US Maritime Law till its revision in 1986. Individual shippers were required to complain to FMC which, after necessary investigation, endeavoured to redress the grievances. Shipping conferences operating in US trades are also under obligation to keep its membership open to any shipping line with requisite capability to provide liner services. Besides, liners are also permitted to operate from outside in competition with the conferences if then so desire. But, every shipping company as a conference or non-conference line providing common carrier service has to file its freight tariff with FMC without whose clearance it cannot canvass business. The FMC examines the structure and level of freight rates and makes sure that they reasonably reflect the cost of providing the liner service and does not involve any restrictive conditions curbing the reasonable freedom and flexibility of the users. The practice of deferred rebate or granting of secret rebates on rates are banned and any breach in this regard invites a heavy fine. No shipping line is permitted to indulge in unfair competition by offering dumping rates or restorting to unethical business practices.

Indian shippers by approaching the MRTPC have, therefore, opened up a veritable Pandora's Box and it would prove a blessing in disguise. Let the MRTPC be armed with necessary statutory powers to deal with the international shipping conferences on the lines of FMC in USA, so that the rules of the game in liner shipping are observed not only by the shipping lines but also the shippers and their spokesmen. Besides, when the Government of India have so far not taken any legal or administrative measures to enforce the provisions of the Liner Code, how can one complain about its violation. The fact of the matter is that for all practical purposes it is not in operation. Moreover, the machinery of consultation which used to exist between the shippers and the Karmahom conference has fallen into disuse, having become redundant in the altered scenario of acute competition and destabilisation of the conference system.

Therefore, the Liner Code which has been ratified by the Government of India and has become operative since October, 1983, will have to be enforced by the Government in the export trades of our country for taking care of the complaint lodged by the shippers. On this count also the shippers have put the Government in the dock. The shippers, shipowners and the concerned Ministries of the Government should clearly know what is in store for them in a situation triggered off by the complaint lodged with the MRTPC.

9

CHEQUERED HISTORY OF LINER CODE

THE MUCH talked about code of conduct of liner Conferences, adopted by UNCTAD in 1974 and which came into force in 1983, is slated to be reviewed in November 1988 by the member countries. The prolonged recession in global shipping caused by the combination of trade recession and uncontrolled expansion of shipping tonnage, has put the code in serious danger. The rationality generated in the attitude of member countries of UNCTAD, developed as well as developing ones, at the time of its adoption now stands totally distorted· The very spirit behind the code is badly vitiated with the change in the global scenario on account of convergence of a number of unexpected and unconducive developments. The weakening of the Conference System under the impact of cut-throat competition reminiscent of the era of pre-conference days, emergence of container technology, substantial growth in the operations of independent liner companies outside the ambit of the institutionalised conferences, entry of speculative operators with questionable practices have given rise to a host of aberrations in the pattern of operation of liner services.

These developments would certainly require not only a review of the situation but also the requisite measures to salvage the form and substance of liner shipping which is expected to provide a common carrier service for a large fraternity shippers in the developed as well as developing countries.

The Review Conference is expected to review the working of the Code with reference to its implementation. But it looks almost certain that some member countries are likely to question the fundamental validity of the code and its relevance in the altered context of the global scenario of shipping. At the same time some member countries are expected to re-emphasise the need for implementation of the code, notwithstanding the adverse developments. The continuing fluid state of international shipping situation lends enough scope for mustering arguments to support the position likely to be assumed by both the sides. Consequently, once again efforts would be on for search of a compromise position acceptable to all member countries on the basis of a broad consensus.

At a micro-level more specific issues would come up for scrutiny. These are: Control and regulation of non-conference or socalled independent operators; need for inclusion of liner cargoes moving on the trade route as a whole; reservation regarding bilateral shipping agreements already in operation; control over the carriage of government cargoes; measures for regulation and control of cargo; booking and canvassing as well as freighting practices; dumping of shipping space at uneconomic level of freight rates and issue of shipping documents in contravention of established business practices and conventions. These issues are likely to prove more vexations and very strong contentions for and against are likely to be maintained by member countries. The perceptions of the developed and developing countries would widely differ in the deliberations of these issues.

The emergence of the container technology and its application has considerably changed the pattern of liner services.

Inter-modalism, feeder network, slot chartering, regional and global services are some of the new and most noticable features, It has rendered the indutstry more capital intensive and developed rigidity of operations with application of a systems approach Obviously the more resourceful developed maritime countries are at an advantage in the matter of faster induction of the technology. This has also conferred more advantages to the developed countries in the conduct of their foreign trade operation and marketing their products with competitive edge. The advantages enjoyed by the developing countires in the traditional items of trade especially in agricultural and agro-based products have already been eroded in many cases by the development of subsitutes in the developed countries. Development and use of modern technology based on advances made in the field of various basic sciences have further widened the gap in the development process and the economic distance between the two group of countries.

In a country like India, it has become possible to develop a fairly modern base for many in dustries by insulating the country through the protective umbrella of import control regime. However, we have allowed a totally free regime so far as the development of commercial shipping industry is concerned. Despite this, through the establishment of a public sector in shipping side by side with the private sector and injection of loan finance through a governmental agency, considerable advances were made in the growth of the national shipping tonnage and development of commercial shipping services.

But the new technological revolution with its massive sweep is rapidly nullifying this progress. The reversal process is also quite visible and inevitable in other developing countries. It has therefore to be realised that international conventions, like the one on the Liner Code, are very necessary for preventing such anomaly in progress and establishment of a new other based on equitable share for all in the field of shipping. As a matter of fact, a similar convention suited to carriage of bulk commodities is also overdue.

It is also absolutely necessary to ponder over the fact during the Review Meeting, on the inordinate delay that occurs in adopting an international convention, its ratification by the governments of the member countries and its implementation. The Liner Code took one decade for adoption and another decade for coming into force and further delays are involved in implementation by the governments of the concerned States. Inevitably, the pressing needs of the situation created by the advances in maritime technology force many countries developed as well as developing, into unilateral actions to preserve and protect their national interests. Thus, the situation keeps on becoming more and more complex and the scops for reaching consensus on the international forum of UNCTAD becomes difficult.

One more dimension to the complex situation has been added by the discussions on trade in service by the member of the GATT, (General Agreement on Trade and Tariffs) an international body to monitor and regulate the international trading system, during the Uruguay Round of negotiations in 1987. Trade in Services including shipping. would now be discussed under the auspices of GATT although separately from those on commodities, under the arrangement of the so-called second track. This is going to have substantial implications and impact on the progress achieved by UNCTAD and the favourable results likely to accrue in future to the developing countries. For example, the developing countries may be forced to sacrifice their interests in the development of services on the bargaining counter of GATT during negotiation on trade in commodities. This would be particularly so in case of trade linked services like shipping, banking and insurance. It is hoped that the implications of the foregoing analysis are borne in mind by the participating delegations of the developing countries in general and India in particular.

10

LENGTHENING SHADOWS ON THE GROWTH OF INDIAN SHIPPING

ON THE basis of available hindsight wisdom in ample measure, our endeavours to produce a viable plan of development for Indian Shipping bristle with difficulties. The ongoing exercise for the Eighth Five Year Plan in this regard would literally hang on the horns of a dilemma. The perspective and paradigm are in confusion with no straight road of future development in sight. The policy of bolting the stable doors after the horses have fled and laxity in finding the key to open the doors when they arrive, has tied us in a knotty situation. While the long recession in the maritime market seeme to have abated, the wreckage of paralysed will to steam ahead is blocking the channel of onward movements.In formulating the objective of the Eighth Plan, the issues to be resolved are basically with regard to the target of tonnage acquisition.

It our planning efforts are for the growth of all vital segments of the economy, as they certainly should be, then it becomes incumbent on our part to reverse the declining trend in the expansion of our shipping tonnage. This process should logically go on till we realise the capability of carrying at least

50 per cent of our bulk trades and 40 per cent of the liner trades. These have been the accepted goals of our policy but require a forced reminder on account of the general diffidence that has developed among our planners, implementing authorities as also the pessimism among the shipping magnates. This is largely on account of the hangover of the prolonged resession in the freight market and our patent inability to control and regulate unfair and wasteful competition on our coasts. Besides, the weak an inadequate information and statistical base with regard to trade movements in terms of quantity and volume, origin and destination and the difficulties in extrapolating the future trends on account of frequent and unpredictable changes in the micro aspects of export and import policies further render the task of preparing a viable development plan difficult. In addition, frequent variations in the modalities for implementation of our trade strategies on account of desperation induced by the balance of payment deficits and influence of powerful trade lobbies, further complicate the overall scenario.

The second important aspect of the task during the Eighth Plan is the deployment of national tonnage with maximum possible utilisation of available capacity. The critical nature of this aspect, will have to be appreciated, considering the highly capital intensive character of investment in ships and the need for fully realising the economies of scale with the increasing size of sea carriers, in the tanker, dry bulk carrier and liner sectors of the industry.

Therefore, while reviewing the physical and financial performance of the national fleet during the Seventh Plan, it would be necessary to bring out the extent of unutilised capacity and the reasons thereof, in terms of laidup ship and vessels operating in different sectors. A closely related aspect in this regard would be the interfacing of the deployment of the national fleet with the target markets overseas and dovetailing of the shipping services with the strategy of export promotion and import facilitation,

This would require an institutionalised machinery involving the representative bodies of trade and shipping for working out the operational implications for the national carriers arising out of major business deals emerging out of the delibrations of the Joint Business Councils, Government-to-Government agreements and bilateral trade and countertrade transactions entered into by the private and the public sector enterprises. It has to be realised that the short notice requirements of trade to odd destinations and cargo specific vessels of bulk items would not be easy to meet without the requisite co-ordination on a continuing basis. The pressure of such requirements is expected to be quite heavy during the Eighth Plan in our auxiety to promote exports through conventional as well as unconventional measures. The demands on Indian Shipping, and particularly on SCI as a public sector enterprise, are likely to be considerable.

The available handling, stuffing/destuffing, storage and local movement facilities, particularly for containerised cargo at our ports and Inland container Depots (ICDs) are further likely to aggravate the problems of shippers, and shipowners with the expected increase in traffic. Before commissioning of new ICDs it would be very necessary to upgrade the functioning of the existing ones through provision of required equipment, streamlining of procedure of clearance and movement of containers, so that Indian Shippers as well as shipowners are in a position to derive full benefits of the container technology on par with their counterparts, expecially in the competing countries. A well planned time-bound programme for industion of this technology which works on the basis of a systems approach has to be put in place to subserve the requirements of our foreign trade operations.

The high cost of handling containerised cargoes especially at the port of Bombay as well as other Ports constitutes one of the biggest disadvantages suffered by Indian shippers. This is basically on account of adhoc and improvised approach in the development of facilities as mentioned earlier. The railways, which hold the primary responsibility for the establishment of the ICDs and fixing of the rail freight tariff, will have to consider on a priority basis the rationalisation of the freight tariff. As a matter of fact the need for making available the benefit of promotional freight rates for the containerised movement of export cargoes which at present constitute captive traffic for the Railways, should be accepted.

The system of receiving containers at our seaports; locally as well as from remote ICDs is at present quite clumsy on account of inadequate backup space at container berths. The stuffing and destuffing operations are being conducted at temporary sites away from the container berths with improvised equipment. Inevitably these would involve multiple and avoidable handling and movements of containers at considerable cost to shippers as well as shipowners. The wage cost of the labour force at our ports further adds on to the total handling cost of containers. Besides, strikes and work-stoppages at our ports, now also ominously spreading to ICDs, further neutralise the efficiency and cost effective characteristics of the container technology.

> Considering the enormous waste of national resources involved because of these factors, there should be no hesitation in imposition of a total ban on such activities under the provisions of the Essential Services Maintenance Act (ESMA). However, if it is considered too drastic a measure in the current sociopolitico climate, let there be a moratorium on such activities over an agreed period of time on the basis of a Memorandum of Understanding (MOU) arrived at between the representatives of port and dock workers and the port authorities and other employment agencies involved in port operations. Such an MOU can also provide for grievance settlement and adjudication machinery to safeguard and protect the legitimate interests of workers.

It is high time to resolve the vexatious question of cargo support for national vessels which alone could provide the basis for a feasible and meaningful policy for any further expansion of the national tonnage during the Eighth Plan. This is not only necessary for the liner tonnage but also for the cargo specific tonnage to be acquired for the bulk trades. The modalities which have surfaced, so far, from different quarters for the purpose will have to be objectively assessed for the benefit of the implementing authorities in the Government. Shippers, organisation have offered the so-called voluntary scheme of providing cargo support duty monitored through its own administive agency, vested with statutory powers and compulsory membership of all shippers. It has also been suggested from some quarters that the patronage of shippers could be secured through a system of direct as well indirect incentives, to which they are accustomed. It is also considered a more effective factor for motivating the Indian Shippers.

A more direct system adopted by some of the developing countries in our neighbourhood is one of giving first preference in patronage to national ships for any shipment, with the option of giving dispensation on the basis of non-availability of their services at the required time, for routes and destinations, as the case may be. This is generally not favoured by Indian shippers since it is considered too drastic and unworkable in the typical Indian conditions. On account of persisting resistance from the trade lobbies reinforced by vested interests with considerable political clouts, a very pragmatic method for cargo support has been evolved by the Ministry of Surface Transport in the form of "Entitlement Voucher Scheme (EVS)." It does not put individual shipments as well as shippers into operational strait jacket of splitting business in the required proportion for conforming to requisite cargo sharing between national and foreign flag vessels. For a smooth change-over the scheme also envisages exemptions for the routes and cargoes not adequately served by the Indian vessels at present. To increase its acceptability among Indian shippers, the provision of matching services at matching rates with those of foreign vessels has also been accepted. Finally, a plan for acquiring 40 per cent share for national ships in a phased manner with a target of 20 per cent to begin with, followed by 30 per cent and ultimately reaching 40 per cent by the end of the Eighth Plan period appears to have been suggested to the user Ministries and Indian shippers.

The prolonged recession in the global shipping market on account of the heavy imbalance between the supply of and demand for shipping space following heavy ordering of tonnage particulary by the developed maritime countries has brought in unethical and unfair commercial practices inculding the cut-throat freight wars spelling the financial doom of many wellestablished shipping companies in the developed as well as developing countries. The latter ones with slender financial resources are the most hard-hit, and cannot afford the waste of financial resources. Under the circumstances, it becomes our paramount responsibility to adopt requisite regulatory measures to restore a health climate for pursuing legimate business activities to facilitate foreign trade operations for those who have a long-term stake in these activities.

> We have allowed the situation to drift too long expecting a self correcting mechanism to emerge. This has not happened and it is high time to act for putting an end to undesirable practices and restoring standard commercial practices. This aspect must receive top priority in our policy formulation so that development planning for this sector of the economy does not get vitiated and prove infructuous. The International shipping scenario has undergone a radical change on account of overtonnaging, entry of speculative operators, high cost of finance, fluctuating exchange rates and a high degree of increased capital investment on account of the economies of scale necessitated by the induction of modern shipping technology. Consequently the element of financial risk and commercial hazards of the shipping business have

increased manifold. These factors are already casting their long and ominous shadows on the existence and development of Indian shipping. It would be, therefore, absolutely necessary to bear in mind their impact in our exercise of planning for the national mercantile marine.

11

STATUS OF SHIPPING IN THE NATIONAL ECONOMY

WHILE considering the fiscal and other customary assistance to shipping, it is very necessary to conceptualise its distinctive nature with regard to development and operations. It has to be recognised that ships are highly tradable assets on account of their international mobility. Therefore, it is very common for a shipping enterprise, especially engaged in tramping operations, to derive profits by timely purchase and sale of ships. However, this is based on the assumption that the purchase and sale activities are relatively free from administrative and procedural constraints.

Shipping is a highly capital in tensive industry and this feature has been greatly intensified under the impact of modern technology which has given rise to the emergence of large bulk carriers, VLCCs and ULCCs for crude oil, specialised product carriers as well as the highly sophisticated container ships. Ipso facto, it follows that a shipping enterprise, especially in a developing country, cannot acquire its fleet wholly from its own capital resources raised through equity. It is therefore quite common to own ships largely on the basis of loan finance, provided by banks and financial institutions, shipbuilders credit as well as through mortgage of long term time charters. This has become possible on accout of the fact that under fairly normal conditions, unlike any other capital intensive industry, there is no gestation period for ships which can commence earn ing freight revenue right from the time of its delivery from the shipbuilding yard. In case of second ships they can be purchased even with revenue earning cargoes already loaded on.

It has also to be recognised that in the case of bulk carriers and tankers, under normal trading conditions, shipowners can recoup their investment within half the useful time of their assets. For the liner ships, this is ensured through assurance of adequate cargo base for liner operations under the established institutional frame work of the conference system on individual trade routes. It may be mentioned here in parenthesis, that this time honoured paradigm was turned upside down on account of the recent prologed recession in the shipping industry on account of a heavy imbalance between the supply and demand factors accentuated by over-tonnaging on the one hand and recession in the movement of trade flows of major items of trade in bulk as well as general cargo sectors on the other. This phenomenon was witnessed on account of a rare combination and convergence of international shipping.

However, the traumatic phase is unlikely to be repeated since shipowners in general and the speculators and over enthusiastic jumpers on bandwagon of new shipping techno-logy have learnt their lessons the hard way in the school of experience. It should not, therefore, vitiate our thinking on the basic nature and operation of commercial shipping activities except that the application of revolutionary new technology has accentuated the risks involved in massive investment of this hazardous industry. We should, therefore. repose our confidence in the development of this industry and reverse the trend of decline in national tonnage to meet the growing needs of foreign trade operations.

The tempo of economic development of our country, builtup during the period of planning of the last seven plans, has not only to be maintained, but has to be accelerated for achieving the target of at least 6 per cent growth in our Gross National Product (GNP) accepted by the Planning Commission on a very conservative basis.

Inevitably this would necessitate developmental imports which have to be paid for by generation of foreign erchange resources through exports. Besides, we have now reached a stage when the repayment of external loan finance and interest thereon, have also begun to exert additional pressure on our foreign exchange resources. Hence, there is the critical need for faster growth of our exports during the Eighth plan and much more so in the subsequent plans till we see the turn of the present century. This challenge on the export front is sought to be met through a strategy of export of production in the thrust areas identified for the purpose along with the thrust markets or target markets. Such a strategy would generate a cargo mix in the movement of our exports and imports consisting of bulk, sembulk and a variety of general cargoes, to and from odd and even destinations all over the globe.

This would necessarily require adequate planning and provision of logistic support from a vast country with a long coastline through development and modernisation of our port system and national merchant marine. Over 90 per cent of our foreign trade moves by the sea route and this would continue to be so in the foreseeable future since only very high value items can afford to move by air. The trade through land frontiers with our neighbouring countries is limited. Besides, sea transport is the cheapest mode of transport especially for dectinations in the overseas markets.

The massive flow of exports and imports to be generated during the next three five-year-plans would require a very dependable and efficient delivery system in a highly competitive international environment. Presently, for many reasons, a large proportion of our seaborne trade both in the bulk and general cargo sectors is carried by foreign vessels, with the lone cxception of crude oil and petroleum products. Inevitably, a sizeable proportion of the freight bill involved in servicing our foreign trade has to be paid in free foreign exchange to non-Indian carriers. The extent of the drain of foreign exchange can be gauged by the annual freight bill in servicing our foreign trade which on the basis of 10 per cent of the currnt level would be over Rs. 3500 crores. Therefore, for improving the balance of payment position on expeditious basis, expansion and better utilisation of national tonnage in the carriage of our overseas trades, become self evident. Besides, for acquiring a measure of self-reliance for providing critical logistic support in maintaining essential supplies in times of civil and military emergencies, adequate tonnage of national shipping fleet is required. Therefore, to adopt a purely accountant's approach while considering investment in national shipping would be highly in appropriate.

It is often not realised, or appreciated, that any export or import transactions, inevitably involve not only the tangible items of merchandise but also the invisible services like shipping, banking and insurance. Therefore, export and import transactions are an inextricable mix of goods and services involving earnings or loss of foreign exchange as the case may be. Shipping services serve a dual purpose. They promote exports and faciliate improts by providing transportation services, to and from, required destinations. In fact they could play a crucial rule in suport of the export strategy and the programme of import planning. Moreover through freight earnings in export and import of merchandise trade they additionally help in augmenting and conserving our foreign exchange resources. For rendering these dual functions, national shipping sector has not been adequately considered for requisite fiscal incentives as compared to the range and magnitude of direct and indirect incentives and assistance provided for promoting merchandise exports.

The major ones are listed below:

(1) Cash Compensatory Support ranging on an average from 10 to 25 per cent on the FOB value of various products for neutrelsing various direct and indirect taxes, cost of penetrating new market, expenditure involved in the development of new products etc. Currently the CCS disbursement would be of the order of anywhere between Rs. 800/- to Rs. 900/- crore of rupees out of the total fund of Rs. 1045/- crores under Market Development Assistance (MDA) provided in the current year's national budget. The remaining amount which is also quite sizeable is disbursed in providing financial support to export promotion institutions, publicity for Indian products, expenses involved in sponsoring trade delegation abroad, trade fair and exhibition.

(2) Substantial amount of revenue loss is incurred in providing customs and excise duty draw backs allowed on input of imported raw-material and components.

(3) Pre-shipment and postshipment finance at almost half the prevailing commercial rate of interest is provided to Indian exportes.

(4) Wholly export oriented enterprises in the six Export Processing Zones (EPZs) and over a hundred Export Oriented Units (EOUs) are virtually free from duties on import of machinery, component parts, raw materials and other accessories. They also enjoy exemptions from local taxes as well as income tax. The latter is now applicable to profits made in export business by the units located in the Domestic Tariff Areas (DTA).

In contrast it has to be noted that the promotional treatment given to shipping industry which is wholly export oriented and also import substituting is quite marginal. Considering its potential for earning and savings of foreign exchange and the crucial logistic support it can provide for the growth of our foreign trade, the fiscal and financial assistance provided is rather inconsequential. Besides, the magnitude of its hazards arising out of heavy capital investment, exposure to intense international competition, perpetual danger of under utilisation of available capacity and lack of any cushion of the domestic market otherwise available to shore based industries would require substantial measures of assistance than hitherto available to Indian shipping enterprises. It may also be added that detention and disruption of shipping services by and large geared to our overseas foreign trade (since crosstrading activities are quite marginal at present) arising on accouut of improvised port infrustructure, frequent bottlenecks in the inland transport system and the usually unsatisfactory state of affairs in our industrial relations at the water front, very adversely affect the efficiency and financial viability of Indian shipping.

The importance of trade in services has been now very well recognised by USA and other developed contries. The question of bringing it within the multilateral system of trade negotiation within GATT framework was, therefore, brought at Punta Del Esta meet during the Uruguay round of trade negotiations. Despite resistance from Brazil, India and other developing countries, negotiation on trade in services which would, among others, inevitably include shipping also, are slated for discussions at the forth coming GATT meet at Montreal in December 1988. It is quite possible that the developing countries when hard pressed for gains on the "merchandise" front may have to give in, on the "Services" front. This would give a heavy blow to the development of service sector for a country like India which to-day is in an advance stage of development. Therefore, before any move for stand-still or maintenance of status quo is made by the developed countries for sevice sector in the matter of giving incentive and assistance by the State, we must act fast in that direction by taking the desirable measures.

12

PRINCE CHARMING'S ROMANCE WITH SHIPPING

THE DEMISE of Dr. Nagendra Singh removes one of the distinguished stalwarts from the national and international shipping scene. He was an acknowledged and renowned expert on international jurisprudence and, more particularly, on maritime law. His interest and association with commercial shipping matters were quite notable during his tenure as Director General of Shipping and, subsequently as Secretary in the erstwhile Ministry of Shipping and Transport, Government of India. Affectionately referred to as Maharaj Saheb in Indian shipping circles, he hailed from the royal family of Dungarpur situated on the border of Rajasthan and Gujarat States. He had many academic accomplishments to his credit and was wellknown for his scholarship and erudite writings. Having been born with a silver spoon in his mouth, he could have easily traded the primrose path of dalliance without leaving the gilded cage. However, this charming prince chose to follow the arduous path of learning and scholarship as well as the administrative responsibility of a civil servant in Independent India.

This columnist had the privilege of working in close association with him during the days of UNCTAD-II meet, held in 1968 at New Delhi. He was the principal member of the Indian delegation participating in the deliberations of the committee on Shipping. The conference lasted for over a month-and-half with prolonged sittings of various committees, day in and day out. In his unassuming style he radiated a rare personal charm while dilating on shipping matters or analysing the splendid facets of various characters of Ramayan and Mahabharata. He was a deeply religious man despite his royal heritage and the bureaucratic powers he wielded in the adminisatrative machinery of the Government of India, wherein his last asignment was in the position of Secretary to the President of India in Reshtrapati Bhawan He could talk with equal ease on the unwieldy nature of international conferences as well as the advantages of taking carrot juice every morning. It is a great pity that such a noble man had to leave this world without heir to himself or to his intellectual legacy.

His devotion and dedication in promoting the cause of Indian shipping need to be recorded by recounting some of the less known but significants incidents. While he was serving his tenure as Secretary in the Ministry of Shipping and Transport, the then management of Scindia Steam Navigation Company, in a desperate bid to redress its grievance, went to a court of law by filling a suit against the Government of India. The provocation arose from the cancellation of the licenses by the DG Shipping of Scindia ships operating on the India-USA Pacific route. This happened during the late sixties, and apparently the reason for doing so seemed to be the fear of over-tonnaging which the DG Shipping was expected to prevent by use of its regulatory power. Scindia's plea was to maintain its right of operation on the route as one of the pioneers of the service against the aggressive entry of the Shipping Corporation of India as a new comer. The decision of DG Shipping was prompted by its anxiety to promote the interest of the public sector shipping enterprise which at that time was in a nascent stage. The action of the Scindia management annoyed Dr. Nagendra Singh, who was then holding the position of Secretary in the Ministry of Shipping. He refused to discuss the matter further with a very senior officer of the Scindia company, then stationed at Delhi. When he happened to meet him in the lift of the Ministry's building, his cryptic remark wes that the matter would be discussed only in the court of law. This would have created quite a crisis and loss of credibility on either side, depending on the verdict of the court. However, thanks to his magnanimity, the Government subsequently restored the licences of the Scindia ships and the creation of an ugly situation was happily prevented.

During the deliberations of the UNCTAD shipping committee he made quite an erudite speech spelling out the role of existing international conventions and practices in the field of shipping and the need for maintaining and strengthening the tradition. The developed countries heartily acclaimed his speech which was interpreted by them as one favouring the maintanance of the status quo. The developing countries which were clamouring for a new International Order in shipping were not very happy with it particularly when they expected a more radical stance on the subject from the Indian Delegation. Considering the strong sentiment of the developing countries on the matter and the importance attached to the position taken by the Indian delegation, Dr. Nagendra Singh was persuaded to deliver one more address on the subject to reiterate the interest and support the common cause of the developing countries. This was done by him so ably and competently without giving even the slightest impression of any shift on India's position.

It also needs to be recorded here that among the several committees which deliberated on the various facets of international trade, transport and other related matters, the accomplishment of the shipping committee turned out to be highly noteworthy. The voice of the developing countries in matters of international shipping, for the first time, came to be recognised by the developed maritime countries. The legitimate need for the development of a merchant marine for developing countries was recognised and the international community agreed to assist them through financial credit and requiste share in the carriage of international trade. The classical position taken by the developed countries that the scarce capital resources of the developing countries should be invested in more profitable and rewarding activities of their economy rather than on shipping was effectively demolished during UNCTAD-II. The crucial and promotional role of national shipping in export promotion strategy and import facilitation for the development of their economies was highlighted quite effectively. Subsequent developments in the international shipping scenario have amply demonstrated the validity of this proposition. The recent phenomenon of prolongned recession in shiping has, as a matter of fact, demonstrated that it is the developed maritime countries which have been extravagant in investing their capital resources by indulging in reckless over tonnaging.

So far as the development of Indian shipping is concerned, it is a pity that we are made to traval back in time and once again reiterate the arguments put forward at the time of UNCTAD-II held two decades ago, before our own policy formulators. The interest and awareness on the subject in official quarters has become diffused. The standard and level of comprehnsion of the subject is now touching almost the bottom line with gradual disappearance of the old timers and stalwarts like Dr. Nagendra Singh, in official as well as nonofficial circles Inter-ministerial wrangles have increased disproportionately in the absence of officers commanding respect and credibility at a senior level. Consequently, the decision making process has become highly dilatory and sterile. Our commitments made on international conventions ratified by the Government of India are not being carried out, to the detriment of the interest of Indian shipping. The overall deterioration in the decision making system and the casualness as well as callousness in implemental actions seem to have reached and intolerable level. This is in sharp contrast to the situation prevailing in sixties. This is highly unfortunate when the tasks before Government demand a much higher degree of proficiency and professionalism. Glowing tributes have been paid to Dr. Nagendra Singh from all quarters, official as well as unofficial, including a well deserved state funeral. It is hoped that the occasion would induce introspection and self appraisal on the part of those who have chosen to pay tributes to the departed soul.

13

WORKING GROUP ON SHIPPING-RITUAL SANS RELIGION

THE PLANNING Commission has constituted a working Group on Shipping in connection with the preparation of the Eighth Five Year Plan (1990-95) in accordance with its customary practice in the past. If the past experience is any guide, the efforts of such Working Group did not have much impact on the policy of the government particularly with reference to implementation and therefore the end results. Of course, in the complex economic and political scenario of our country, it is always easy to discover scapegoats for not realising the stated targets and goals. Therefore, such exercises undertaken by the administrators and experts have proved to be more ritualistic without realisation of the substance of the religion. This apprehension is hoisted in the hope of a better experience this time than in the dismal past. Excepting on the port front, the performance in terms of planning, development and deployment of shipping tonnage has been a total disaster so far as the Seventh Plan is concerned. As a matter of fact the fatlure in performance began since the Sixth Plan. The shipping tonnage target of 7.5 million GRT fixed for the Sixth Plan could not be realised. In fact a negative trend in the growth of tonnage was witnessed. With the flagging spirit, the planners, therefore, fixed the same tonnage target for the Seventh Plan. This is also not likely to be realised. But the supreme tragedy has been the liquidation of a number of Indian Shipping Companies including the great Scindia. The postmortem analysis, of the disaster, made by the official quarters laid blame on the worldwide recession in shipping and the modus operandi followed in loaning operations of the Shipping Development Fund Committee. (SDFC), which was abolished with effect from 5th April, 1987. A new Ship Acquisition Licencing Committee has been setup to process acquisition of ships. The financial assistance function is being discharged now by the Shipping Credit and Investment Corporation of India (SCICI). So far as the Shipping Corporation (SCI) in the public sector is concerned the Ministry of Surface Transport and the relevant department of the Ministry of Finance deal with these matters. Besides, The Government has setup a high level Inter-Ministerial Committee to monitor problems of and suggest remedial for the shipping industry. It holds regular dialogue with the industry and reviews the domestic as well as international situations.

While dilating upon phenomenon of global recession in shipping industry the MOST Annual Report (1986-87) states "Almost from the close of 1974 the shipping industry the world over slumped following the hike in oil prices and consequent cut-back in production with too many ships chasing the progressively falling quantum of cargo. Indian shipping industry has not been an exception to this phenomenon. Government have been making continuous assessement of factors, responsible for the present slump in Indian shipping Industry. The main contributory factor is want of adequate liner trade and bulk cargo aggravated by continuous increase in expenditure in ship operating costs".

"The technological change that has overtaken the world shipping during last few years has had its effect on Indian shipping. While containerisation of general cargo has engulfed almost all trades with the developed countries, India is yet to own a sizeable fully containerised cellular fleet. This has led to the following consequences:

(i) Competition from non-conference lines in general cargo trades on all most all routes. For foreign lines Indian's trade is wayport trade and therefore such lines are able to offer lower freight rates which often do not have co-relation to costs of operations; and

(ii) Lack of containerised carrying facilities with Indian lines. It is only now that the three major Indian lines have formed a consortium to provide direct container services on fornightly basis to the continents etc."

The Working Group's very first terms of reference is to review the financial and physical performance of shipping during the Seventh Plan period, with particular reference to the Plan targets and draw lessons therefrom for the Eighth Plan. The diagnosis of the crisis as made by the Ministry is at best sketchy and facile. One is not sure about magnitude of the impact of global economic recession. Time and again it has been mentioned in this column that the recession in global trade has at best partial impact. This is very clear from progressive increase in the volume of cargo handled by our major ports, year after year, even after taking into account some amount of double counting due to coastal movements. The second factor to be kept in view for correcting our perspective is the fact that Indian shipping tonnage is basically deployed in the overseas trade of the country barring a marginal amount of cross-trading which become incidental to international shipping operations. The third aspect in this context related to containerisation. It has to be recognised that with scarce capital resources and abundance of labour force employed at our major ports, our marriage with highly capital intensive container technology has been that of a reluctant brids with plentiful tears in the eyes. Since the foreign buyers increasingly insist supply of cargo in containers to which their physical distribution system, inventory control and accounting system are geared, we are willy-nilly forced in the induction of this technology. Besides, there is scarcity of labour force for discharge operations of break-bulk cargo at ports in the developed countries. What ever limited facilities available at these ports are very expensive on account of high labour cost for handling break-bulk cargoes. Consequently, the induction of container technology in India is largely on account the push are pressures of external factors.

The Ministry's annual report clearly admits that "As regards cargo support to Indian Shipping Companies, India does not have any scheme to provide cargo support to its liner shipping industry. However, the following steps have been taken to increase the share of Indian shipping companies:

(a) With a view to ensuring greater share of cargo for Indian Vessels India has entered into bilateral Shipping agreements which provide for parity in cargo lifting and freight earnings.

(b) There are standing instructions to Public Sector Undertakings/Government Departments to negotiate as far as possible, C & F exports and FOB imports. These are designated to maximise cargo availability to Indian Lines.

(c) Share of Indian Shipping Lines in the carriage of Iron Ore exported by MMTC has been brought up through successful commercial negotiations.

(d) The use of foreign flag vessels in the oil trade has been brought down by arranging acquisition of suitable tankers for Indian Shipping Companies.

(e) Beside above steps, fiscal benefits to the shippers inducing them to use Indian bottoms are given by the Ministry of Commerce. At present the following two benefits are being given to shippers for this purpose:

 (i) The freight paid shall not be debited to the face value of import licence if the Ocean freight is paid in non-convertible rupees in India and the goods are carried on Indian Vessels and;

(ii) In case of export shipments carried from Indian Port in Indian vessels to discharge Ports in overseas markets the exporters will be given the REP licence on the exports in question at the rate of 10 per cent higher than their normal replacement rate *i.e.* 11 per cent as against the normal rate of 10 per cent and so on.

The overall share of Indian ships in the carriage of our overseas cargo for the year 1986-87 worked out to about 37 per cent (provisional) on the basis of information received from major and minor ports. Prima Facie, this assessment is misleading since it merely measures the share of national bottoms in terms of volume only. What is more important and relevant is our share in the total freight revenue accrued annually in servicing the foreign trade of the country. This would be much lower than 37 per cent volume share and it is time to device ways and means of its computation since it would serve a better guide for the policy formulators.

It is also a pity that the concerned Ministry is obliged to make a bald statement that we do not have any scheme for cargo support to national bottoms engaged in liner shipping. This is followed by a rank straightfoward platitude that "The matter regarding cargo reservation for Indian Flag vessels as also adoption of the U.N. liner Code is under adive consideration of the Government". It is rather intriguing not to find any reference or record about the intensive efforts made by the Ministry in this regard, expecially in terms of evolving one of the most ingenious device that would be acceptable to our administrative culture and the exporting community mostly consisting of medium and small exporters. This is the over-debated "Entitlement Voucher Scheme". Perhaps, this was designed to save possible embarrassement arising out of the failure to implement the scheme and bringing into open the opposition of the lobbies of vested interests, aided and abetted by the Ministries representing the ship users. The steps enumerated to increase the share of Indian Ships read like a testament of pubiic apology since none of them have contributed anything substantial to save the Indian shipping companies from extinction or to stop the declining trend in the growth of Indian tonnage.

The reference about the contribution of bilateral shipping arrangement in this regard is now historical. It was done over 25 years ago particularly at the instance of the Government of USSR. The standing instructions to public sector undertakings and government departments are often honoured in breach rather that in conformity. It has taken over two decades for MMTC to secure about 25 to 30 per cent share for national ships in the carriage of iron ore to Japan. The sizeable increase in the carriage of crude oil and petroleum products by the national tanker fleet is largely on account of two major factors *viz.*, (a) Critical nature of import input to feed the refinaries and (b) reluctance of foreign tankers to get involved in the hazardous operations on account of the prolonged armed conflict between Iran and Iraq. With regard to the incentives offered by the Ministry of commerce they are very marginal in their impact and are extremely inadequate to provide any tangible and positive motivation for patromising national ships.

It is pretty clear from above that there is no dearth of ideas and blueprint of measures to resolve our problems arising on account of domestic constraints or adverse forces operating in the international environment. Our major weakness is the lack of adequate and effective implementation. The administrative machinery of the government is often paralysed by over working lobbies of vested interest. The lowering of the general standard of the governance of the country has also fallen over years as also the weakening of the political will to implement the decisions taken for safeguarding the overall interest of the country.

The terms of reference of the Working Group also state about physical targets and financial outlays, requirements for replacement, modernisation and fresh acquisition, and training of maritime personnel. The issues required to be considered are:

(a) The need to make shipping financially viable and self-sustaining;

(b) technological developments;

(c) need to improve our liner and bulk cargo share;

(d) need for diversification of Indian shipping into related activities and acquisition of special vessels; and

(e) need for reorientation of training programmes to suit ship technology. The Working Group is also charged with the following tasks:

To determine productivity norms and suggest measures to improve the structural, operational and organisational productivity of Indian Shipping.

To recommend policy measures on fiscal, institutional and operational aspects, conducive to the development of the industry on a sound commercial basis.

To evaluate foreign exchange eardings and outgo of shipping and the likely not earning in the Eighth Plan.

To give broad guidelines for an integrated transport system, development of coastal shipping, sailing vessels, minor and intermediate ports and inland water transports, etc.

The Planning Group on Shipping and the Major Ports Reforms Committee have exhaustively dealt with most of these aspects and issues stated above. Their reports were submitted to the government only in the recent past. In view of this let the members of the group process the information already available for implementing the recommendations already made. There is no estensible purpose in forgetting these reports so soon. It would save a lot of time and efforts of the Working Group to do so.

14

SHIP'S FEMININE GENDER FUNCTIONAL FOR CARRYING CARGO

It Is quite interesting and often enlightening experience to go into the genesis of the customary usage of expressions and terminologies very common to shipping operations. The British Shipowners have done some pioneering work in this regard during their heydays. In the English language, which has become virtually the language of shipping, a ship is assigned the feminine gender for very good reasons. Firstly its operations being highly dependent on the elements of nature, it often tends to be a creature of moods. Secondly, it has to carry (cargo and men) which is a function assigned by Nature to the female of the species. Likewise, if we accept the above propositions, than the next terminology *viz.*, "Husbanding of the Vessel" when it arrives at a port becomes quite logical. This columnist does not intend to indulge in any exercise of lexicography without a purpose.

Some of the leading shipowners, by and large, engaged in tramping trade have been emphasising persistently in the press and on various forums, the need for fiscal incentives without any over reference to measures conducive to the availability of cargoes.

Traditionally, the tramping sector is governed generally by the competitive forces of supply and demand operating in the shipping market and it is as sumed that shipowners have to fend for themselves for the cargo. Shipowners all over the world as well as in India know too well that the so-called competitive market forces are often vitiated by control over cargoes secured through horizonal and vertical integration of interests between large shipowners, especially tanker owners, oil producing companies and transnationals involved in mining operations, and foodgrains production. Besides, speculators, operating at various centres of international charter markets often succeed in manipulation of market forces for inflating or depressing the tramp freight rates to subserve their group interest. Therefore, there are obvious hurdles in getting access to cargo in cross trade by the bulk carrier/tanker fleet of developing countries.

The advantages of having crew and officers at favourable manning scales are fast disappearing on account of the facilities and concessions offered by the FOC countries to shipowners of developed maritime countries and the growing demand for higher wages and salaries by those employed on the fleet of developing countries. Increasing degree of automation of modern technology oriented but capital intensive vessels largely owned by the developed countries further weakens the competitive strength of the developed countries.

Therefore, it is almost axiomatic that the nascent fleets of developing countries have to preforce fall back upon the bulk cargoes generated in the trades of their own countries. And the need in this regard become more pressing with acquisition and deployment of tonnage of larger size for remaining cost effective and competitive in shipping operations.

Under the circumstance the developing countries since 1968 on the forum of UNCTAD have been clamouring for the right of at least carrying 50 per cent of the bulk cargo exports originating and imports terminating in their countries. It must not be forgotton that basic viability of the operations of a ship, in the ultimate analysis, has to be ensured on the basis of the sound British dictum that the ship's feminine gender is functional to carry cargo.

Therefore, while granting full credit to the business acumen and management skill displayed by some of our shipping enterprises in the private sector, it has to be recognised that during the crisis period of recession, their financial viability has been largely sustained on account of the availability of bulk cargoes moving on government account. Particular mention may be made in this regard of the import of crude oil and petroleum products at freight rates based on cost-plus-basis formula, accepted by the Indian Oil Corporation. Besides, ONGC operations have also provided them with the opportunity of operating OSV vessels, as an additional avenue of profitable business. It is also not unusual to find them veciferous in their demand for commitment of bulk cargoes like chemical for employment of specialised tonnage owned and operated by these companies.

For the well known reasons analysed above, there is nothing wrong with this. However, it willynilly proves that expansion and maintenance of our nascent fleet cannot be accomplished merely on the basis of fiscal incentives. If liner shipping operations required an adequate cargo base so also the tramping operations, particularly in the context of a developing country which is very much vulnerable to the damaging influence of speculative operators in international business. It has also to be noted here that the Indian Delegation with the support of other developing countries has maintained, during the recent Montreal meet of GATT, that while negotiating on services, their development aspect has to be taken into consideration, keeping in view the needs of the developing economies. In the services sector of trade, this is far more valid for shipping as one of the directly linked services with the international trade in merchandise.

Therefore, those who are really worried about our balance of payments position may well advised to enlarge their focus beyond our trade in merchandise. We must stretch our sovereign right to adequately participate in the carriage of our foreign trade.

Likewise, it is also necessary to remove the false perception of those advocating lower equity-debt ratio for shipping companies since the one adopted by SDFC (1:6) was supposed to have pushed many enterprises into the red and eventually leading to their winding up. It has to be recognised that for a highly capital intensive industry like shipping it is customary as well as necessary to have acquisition of the fleet largely on the basis of loan finance generally secured from shipbuilders through credit sales, national financial institutions and commercial banks in India as well as abroad. Loan finance constitutes a special feature of the shipping industry, since it suits both the receivers as well as suppliers on account of the fact that ships being internationally mobile assets are conveniently sold and purchased in the global market. And more importantly they have the capability of generating freight revenue without any gestation period. Besides, in generally favourable market conditions, shipowners can recoup the original price of ships within half the active life span of the asset. It is also quite common to raise bank credit against mortgage of long-term time charters of bulk carriers and tankers.

With regard to the liner sector of shipping, for over a century the institution of Shipping Conferences/Freight Agreement Associations virtually provided commercial an economical viability to liner services committed in advance on the basis of a reasonably assured cargo base on a given trade route. Therefore, the equity-debt ratio of 1:6 accepted by SDFC in the past, for the purpose of providing loan finance for developing the nascent fleet of the country, does not lend any scope for criticism. It is the unusually prolonged recent recession in global shipping which has turned the situation upside down and distorted our perception on the development and operation of the national mercantile marine. Over-tonnaging indulged in by the shipowners of developed maritime countries aided and encouraged by extensive shipbuilders credit and speculative finance together with availing of the facilities offered by the flag-of-convenience countries provided them with the completely wrong signals and directions on the proverbial mariner's compass. We, in the developing countries can not afford to play the game on the distorted rules of the developed countries. The international conventions as well as practices provide us with enough latitude to promote and protect our development and expansion of mercantile marine through legal and administrative means based on understanding with developed, developing and socialist countries. By not doing so, we have lost opportunity of acquisition of tonnage available at half the normal price and the opportunity of taking advantage of the buoyant market for lack of adequate tonnage. It is high time to realise the conceptual error being committed by the policy formulators, on jumping to erroneous conclusion, in context and experience of recession. Besides, the usual limitation of acting on so called hindsight wisdom often tantamounts to bolting the stable after the horses have fled.

15

OBSERVATIONS ON PRESS COMMENTS

I

YOUR comments on cargo support (Facts and Facets, ET June 10) are very topical and timely. However, the surmise that the trade is allowed to operate on "catch as catch can" basis is not at all appropriats. Quite often facts are stranger than fiction and facets are more intriguing to understand.

The rationale for cargo support emanates from the provision of the liner code adopted in 1974 on the forum of UNCTAD, on the basis of the consensus that the nascent shipping fleets of developing countries require a legitimate participation and share in the carriage of its oversees liner trades for ensuring viable operations. The code which has come into operation since October, 1983 leaves it to the ratifying countries to enforce the provisions in this regard through legal and/or administrative means. In the typical Indian situation, the shippers on the trade interests and their representative organisations really do not subscribe to the concept of cargo support to national carriers although a lot of lip sympathy is paid in the press and on public platforms. The covert and overt opposition to cargo support has enhanced after the institution of shipping conferances became weak and the liner freight rates virtually became negotiable in the wake of recessionary conditions and emergence of cut-throat competition among shipping lines. The situation gave a body blow to a number of old and established shipping companies especially operating in the liner treades. For the shippers also, the "catch as catch can" situation gave short term benefits on wholly arbitrary basis. Larger shippers benefits more on account of the leverage of business and the intermediaries lop off the benefits that would otherwise accrue to medium and small shippers. The situation also gave rise to unethical and unfair business practices detrimental to national interest.

It is pertinent to dispel common confusion between tramp shipping usually operating within the framework of market forces and liner shipping providing common carrier service. The latter has definite obligations in terms of providing adequate, stable and scheduled services to designated ports with stability of foreight rates at least in short and medium period, for meeting the requirement of numerous shippers. Services and shipping space are committed in advance without any commitment of cargo from shippers. Therefore sustainance of liner services is, if so facto, dependent on cargo support of the shippers. Intardependence based on autuality of interest has therefore, to be racognised if trade in general cargo has to be promoted on the basis of common carrier liner services. Any indulgence in "catch as you catch can" is tatolly inconsistent with the operational logic of liner shipping.

II

While I very much appreciate Sneh Lata Bhatia's report entitled "Legislation Recognising CTDs in the Offing" (ET. 5th September) Date Line, New Delhi, it is necessary to point out that she has missed the focus of the legislation necessitated in the wake of induction of container technology in our country.

Containerisation today is the state of the art technology for the movement of liner cargoes in the international trade,

Developing countries including India, are not readily prepared for the induction of this highly capital intensive and labour displacing technology on accouut of scarce financial resources and a large labour force employed at our ports. However, we are virtually pushed into it, largely on account of external factors. Foreign buyers increasingly demand cargo in containers since their physical distribution system, inventory control and financial accounting are geared in terms of container units Besides, ports in the developed countries have now very limited facilities for handling of the conventional break-bulk cargo on account of high cost of scarce labour. Consequently, we have responded to the situation by resorting to improvisation in provision of infrastructure facilities at requir various inland containers depots and major container handling ports. It has not been realised that the technology based on a systems approach is not amenable to improvisation. Likewise, the prevailing legal regime applicable to movement, handling and shipment of export cargoes requires suitable modifications for facilitating the functioning of the inter-modal system of transportation which is the hallmark of this technology. Therefore, the conventional concept of deemed export after the goods have left the teritorial waters of India, under existing provisions of the Indian Customs Act, the amount of liability assumed by the sea-carriers for loss or damage to cargo and the containers, the non-acceptance of the responsibilities of a bailes by the railways etc., have to be changed and brought into conformity with the internationally prevailing norms and practices. The Combined Transport Document (CTD) on the Combined Transport Bill of Lading issued at various ICDs in India to shippers of export cargoes, is a heavily improvised version of its counterpart elsewhere in the world. This was done so on account of our habit of indulging in adhocism and resorting to easy options by obviating the efforts needed for necessary changes in the legal regime. Consequently the CTD, although has been designed as a bankable document is not acceptable to foreign buyars of Indian goods and in most cases they refrain from its inclusion among the documents to be collected against payment to exporters under the Letter of Credits arrangements made with the banks in India. Therefore, the move to evolve a CTD with internationally acceptable terms and conditions is most welcome. But the improvised infrastructure for movement and handling of containers and transport bottleneck in the inland movement of containers would continue to reduce the dependability of our system and credibility as well as confidence of foreign buyers. It has also to be noted that the shipping companies would continue to assume the responsibility of a Combined Transport Operator (CTD) in the typical situation of our country. It is too early to think of freight forwarders or Non Vessel Owning Common Carriers (NVDCC) to come in the picture as CTD, as envisaged under the International Convention on Multimodal Transport adapted in 1980 by the international community, which has not yet come into force. While the government machinary habitually moves slow and only under the pressure of the law of gravitation, the plans for proliferation of more ICDs would aggrevate the difficulties of not only the exporters but also the sea-carriers and anybody who wants to assume the responsibilities of CTD.

III

This has reference to your editorial on "40 per cent no answer" (ET, Sept. 22), which smacks of faulty perception fallacious reasoning, right from the very first sentence. You have stated, "The academic approach of the surface transport ministry in pleading for 40 per cent cargo reservation for Indian liner shipping has been exposed by the commerce and other ministries as impracticable." Thereafter references are made about the inability of Scindia to modernise, inadequate services of India Steamship and incapability of SCI to provide efficient service. According to you the fault lies with the licensing norms pursued by the Ministry of Surface Transport. The immediate remedy suggested is to provide a subsidy to the companies till they could stand on their own feet. And finally it is stated "Indian Shipping should go ahead with an action plan for modernisation if Indian bottoms are to play a dominant role. . . ". This is an excellent exercise in over simplification of the problems of the industry, not undertaken hopefully for want of space available in your columns. Conceptually, liner shipping represents a common carrier service wherein the shipping space has to be committed well in advance without any prior commitment of cargo patronage from the shippers. Utilisation of the committed cargo space for each sailing declared therefore becomes a critical factor. This aspect got further accentuated with the emergence of container ships having three to four times the capacity of conventional vessels. Overtonnaging in the wake of containerisation in the liner trades of the world, has brought in cut-throut competition resulting in colossal waste of resources and liquidation of some of the most reputed shipping companies in Europe, USA and even Japan. In the very nature of things, therefore liner shipping services of the nascent fleet of developing countrie s can not be sustained under these circumstances. It has to be understood that the type of competition based on market forces of supply and demand suited to tramping services for movement of bulk cargoes is illsuited to dedicated and committed common carrier services. The tramp ships are contract carriers and are hired on the basis of quantity of cargo actually available for shipment and negotiated freight rates. The quality of servie and abequacy of space in liner shipping services would necessarily depend upon the overall viability of service based on availability of cargo or in other words cargo support provided by the shippers to services which have to be scheduled in advance for the convenience of the users. Therefore, for the development and growth of liner shipping services of the developing countries, cargo support measures become inevitable. It is precisely on this rationale that the UNCTAD adopted the liner code with provision of minimum 40 per cent cargo support after a very comprehensive and exhaustive examination of the subject. To question this proposition is therefore totally ill-advised and redundant. Your editorial on the subject betrays reasoning of a very casual nature and it is rather unusual for the paper of your standing. It will be highly appreciated if this issue is thrown open to debate among the readers of your paper.

IV

This has reference to your comments about SCICI lending in Facts and Facets feature (ET of 5th November). You have stated, "The demand of shipowners is that the present debt-equity ratio of 1:3 for loans on ship acquisition be relaxed to 1:6. This was being done by the erstwhile SDFC. No wonder that such a liberal policy of SDFC pushed the organisation into red eventually leading to its winding up". You have therefore, justified the reluctance of the Ministry of Finance to concede the Indian shipowners demand in this regard so that SCICI does not get into the difficulties of loan recoveries from the shipping companies. Firstly, it should be equity-debt ratio and not the otherway around as you have stated. It has to be recognised that for a highly capital intensive industry like shipping it is customary as well as necessary to have the acquisition of the fleet largely on the basis of loan finance generally secured from shipbuilders through credit sales, national financial institutions and commercial banks in India as well as abroad. Loan finance constitutes a special feature of the shipping industry since it suits, both the receivers as well as suppliers on account of the fact that ships being internationally mobile assets are convenient to sell and purchase and are capable of generating freight revenue without any gestation period. Besides in a generally favourable market conditions shipowners can recoup the original price of the ships within half the active life of the asset. It is also quite common to raise bank credit against mortgage of long-term time charters of the bulk carriers and tankers. With regard to the liner sector of shipping, for over a century the instiution of Shipping Conferences/Freight Agreement Associations, virtually provided commercialy and economicaly viable operations on the basis of a reasonably assured cargo base on a given trade route. Therefore, the equity-debt ratio of 1:6 accepted by the SDFC in the past, for the purpose of providing loan finance for developing the nascent fleet of the country, does not lend any scope for criticism. It is the unusually prolonged recent recession in shipping which has turned the situation upside down and distorted our perception on the development and operation of national mercantile marine. Over tonnaging indulged in by the shipowners from developed maritime countries by extensive use of speculative finance and availing of the facilities offered by flag of conveniance countries have provided them with completely wrong sinnals and directions on the proverbial mariner's compass. We in the developing countries can not afford to play the game on the distorted rules of the developed countries. The international conventions as well as practicies provide us with enough latitude to protect our development and expansion of mercantile marine through legal and administrative means based on understanding with developed, developing and socialist countries. By not doing so we have lost opportunity of acquisition of tonnage available at half the normal price and now opportunity of taking advantage of the buoyant market for lack of adequate tonnage. It is high time to realise the conceptual error being committed by the policy formulators, on jumping to erroneous conclusions in the context and experience of the recession. Besides, the usual limitation of acting on, so called hindsight wisdom often tantamounts to bolting the stable after the horses have fled.

It is also necessary to provide timely fiscal incentives by recognising shipping as saver and earner of foreign exchange. Before our hands are tied behind our back during the GATT negotiations on services, we must also initiate measures for cargo support in terms of legitimate proportion. Implemental actions have to follow simultaneously on both the fronts to resolve impasse faced by Indian shipping. If this is not understood, nothing worthwhile could be understood, in the official quarters.

16

THE SAGA OF VIETNAM—TRADE AND TRASPORT CRUCIAL TO DEVELOPMENT

HISTORIAN of the past while recognising the future potentials, used say that China was a sleeping giant. This columnist's recent sojourn for a month in the Socialist Republic of Vietnam (S.R. Vietnam—as mentioned in all official documents) leads to a similar reaction, but with an important variation. Vietnam today is a fully awakened leopord, with the killer instinct developed against the enemies of the country during 40 years of war, fought against the French imperialist power and subsequently against US intervention made for rolling back the emerging force of a socialist government. The magnitude of devastation and distruction it suffered could be gauged from the fact that at one stage the US government spent a hefty sum of US $ 30 billion annually on its operations in the Vietnam war and the amount of bombs dropped in that country exceeded the quantity used during World War II. Any other country would have been virtually wiped out under the impact of such a prolonged on slaught. But its instinct foı survival is incredible. With the return of peace and unification of the country in 1975, the restoration and reconstruction process of the wartorn country began. Now the leapord's killer instinct is being diverted to rapid economic development of the country The government and people of Vietnam are in great urnest to makeup for the time lost on account of the prolonged war. There is a legitimate hurry to catchup with other countries, on the economic front by a quantum jump.

Its economy is essential agricultural and endowed with minoral resources like coal, tin, bauxite, some amount of graphite and oil bearing off-shore areas in the Southern Coast of the country. Major agricultural crops are rice, maize, tea, coffee, jute, tobacco, groundnuts, sugar cane and rubber. These items, therefore, generally figure prominently in its export trade. The country has been able to develop industries to an extent to produce machine tools, cement, agricultural machinery, paper, rubber products, textiles, soap, detergents, and small boats. Shrimp and fishery products, canned fruits and vegetables, edible oil, cashew nuts, wood and wood products leather and leather products, as well as handicrafts constitute important items of exports with considerable growth potentials.

However, the economic development of the country, inevitably, requires rapid industrialisation of the country, for raising the living standard of the Vietnamese prople through generation of employment opportunities for the population currently estimated between 60 to 65 million. Raising of income levels and increase in the availability of goods and services are required to improve the quality of life. The process of industrialisation has necessitated large scale imports of plants and machinery, components and spare parts, indcstrial raw materials, fertilisers, transport vehicles, fuels, and consumer durables like refrigerators, T.V., electric appliances and electronic goods.

Vietnam, like any other developing country but in much more acute form currently suffers from a heavy deficit in its balance of trade The import bill of the country continues to rise far more rapidly than he revenue generated by exports. At present exports earnings can take care of only 40 percent of the annual payment liability on account of its imports. The development process of the country has given rise to higher level of imports which cannot be sastained at the existing level of exports except on the basis of financial assistance from friendly countries. But for sustaining and accelerating rapid strides of industrialisation, the country will have to augment its exports to pay for growing exports, at a much faster rate.

A high level of domestic inflation and a heavy depreciation of the external value of its currency, are further aggraviating the imbalance between value of imports and exports of the country. This is sought to be corrected by the government by opening out doors of the national economy for attracting foreign investment and induction of modern tehnology. The promulgation of the New Law of Investment in Vietnam, is a positive step in that direction. It is expected that the liberal provisions of the law would promote faster development of the economy. This has also to be, inevitably accompanied by accele-ration in the growth of exports based on industrial growth and special export promotion measures. In course of time, it is quite reasonalble to expect a change in pattern of the composition and direction of export from Vietnam. In the terminology of trade, it would mean diversification of exports in terms of products and destination markets. As the level of industrialisa-tion goes up, more value added products would figure in the export trade of the country. A number of new products would emerge along with the traditional agricultural and mineral commodities. Based on the present trend in the government policy, it is also expected that Vietnam would also have to enter into trade, substantially, with market economy countries, while maintaining its established trade linkages with socialist and other friendly countries. All these are bound to generate a heavy demand on its truncated transport infrastructure, now recovering from the ravages of the war.

Geographically, Vietnam is strategically situated in the South East Asian region. It has a long coastline of 2000 Kms facing the Eastern Sea and Gulf of Tonking. The former Indo-China eventually got divided into Vietnam, Laos and Kampuchea (farmer Combodia). It has common border with

Laos, Kampuchea and China. The foreign trade of the country is served by nine important sea ports *viz.*, Campha, Hongai, Haiphong Cualo, Danang, Quinhon, Nhatrang, Saigon and Vungtau situated in the Northern, Central and Southern parts of the country. Saigon port attached to the Hochin Minh City is the most important and welknown port historically developed by the French with a string of 10 berths and dry docking and repair facilities for small vessels. The entire port system of the country needs. Considerable expansion to cope up with growing traffic and is under an urgent need of modernisation of the cargo handling equipments. The landlock country of Laos is served by the port of Haiphong and some amount of traffic for Kampuchea is handled by the central Vietanmese ports for logistic reasons. The curved horn shape of the country also needs strengtherning of the rail and road connection for the North-South and South-North movement of traffic. Presently most of the foreign trade traffic moves with transhipment at Singapore.

All shipping activities in the Socialist Republic of Vietnam are directed by the Ministry of Communication and Transport (MOCT). The Ministry has a separate Vietnam General Maritime Department (Gemadept) to control the activities of all shipowners, shipping agents, ports shipbuilding and repairs. The Ministry has under its direct administrative control but independent management, Vietnam chartering and shipbroking corporation (Vietfracht). Its main function are shipbroking, chartering of vessels and booking of shipping space and providing regular services in the following trades with a small fleet of six chartered vessels with dead weight capacity ranging between 1100 tons. to 1600 tons:

1. Vietnam—Japan—Vietnam: 45 days per sailing
2. Saigon—Singapore—Saigon: 15 days per sailing
3. Saigon—Hongkong, Taiwan, Japan and back: monthly sailing for refeer cargoes.

4. Tramping services with the help of two vessels to Japan South Korea, Indonesia and philippines for carriage of steel scrap, coal, fertilisers, cement rice etc.

It has representative offices at London, Singapore, Sofia (Bulgaria), Rostock, Budapest, and Gdynia, and agents at Hongkong, Singapore, Tokyo, Bangkok, London and Autwerp.

Another state owned company, Vietnam Ocean Shipping Company (VOSCO) has a fleet of 20 vessels with dead-weight capacity ranging from 5600 tons to 16000 tons. These ships flying vietnamese flag are trading between vietnam and Europe. Some of them also call at Asian ports, especially, in Thailand, Singapore, Hongkong, Taiwan, Japan and even South Korea. Philippines and Indonesia are through voyage charter services. The Vietnam Sea Transport and chartering Company (Vitrans-chart) have a fleet of 21 vessels with dead weight capacity ranging between 2600 tons to 16000 tons. They fly the Panamanian Flage (presumable chartered vessels) and call at European and Asian ports. The Vietnam Shipping Company (Vinaship) has fleet of 30 ships with dead weight capacity ranging from 750 tons to 12000 tons. Its main function is to serve the coastal trade of the country, consisting of goods and passengers. When required they deviate to overseas trade and call at Hongkong, Singapore and Japan. Besides, these state owned companies, there are also about fourteen local small shipping enterprises such Quinicoship, Maritrans, Hamatco, Rimotco, Danasco etc.

The foreign shipping lines operating in Vietnamese overseas trades are Fisco and Black Sea from USSR, Polish Ocean line, DSR line, a Bulgarian line, Interlighter and the CGM. USSR lines provide feeder services, two monthly sailings from Haiphong, Danang and Saigon with the use of four container-ship of 300 TEUs and few conventional and combi ships. Besides, a fleet of 10 Vietnamese tankers with the deadweight capacity ranging from 1000 to 20,000 tones along with the

Soviet petroleum product carriers and Japanese crude oil carriers endeavour to meet its requirement of oil traffic.

Considering the crucial role of shipping and ports in the management of foreign trade, there is a strong desire to seek assistance and help in these field from co-developing and friendly countries like India, through collaborations and joint ventures. The country is also eagerly looking for training of sea-cadets, officers and management personnel for shipping and ports.

Vietnam is a country with a great future destiny. Its war-hardened and disciplined people are marching forward with what ever meagre means available to them, if no body is found walking in the streets of Los Angelese where. everybody owns a car, nobody is found walking in the streets of Hanoi since every body moves on cycle. Capacity to do hard work under the worst possible conditions with a smile on the face is the most noticable trait of the Vietnamese. Perhaps they know the value of life much move than people in other countries who have not passed through the trauma of a prolonged and devastating war. One of the blessings in disguise of the war is the large-scale entry of their women folk in civil and economic administration of the country. This became inevitable since most men were engaged in defence effort of the country. The emergence of a strong and experienced women power is one of the great assets of the otherwise poor country. After all Mao used to say that women hold half the sky. The great veteran leader Hochin Minh who died in 1968 but almost preserved lifelike still continues to be the rallying force far people of Vietnam. He died a bachelor and considered people of Vietnam as his childern.

17

IMPLICATIONS OF GATT NEGOTIATIONS ON SERVICES FOR NATIONAL SHIPPING

The Government of USA perhaps deserves lefthanded compliments for generating awareness on the importance of trade in services, now being brought virtually under negotiations of GATT. The developing countries could not succeed in their move to forestall it during the Urguey round of trade negotiation at *Punta del Este*. in September 1986. The US approach in the currently, on going Geneva negotiations on the subject should also put the developing countries on a "Red Alert" for protecting their legitimate interests. The two cardinal aspects which have to be kept in view: *viz*., the end objective of these negotiations is to secure liberalisation of the service sector by the interests which play a dominant role in international trade in services rather than in merchandise and precisely for this reason the developing countries, wherein the service sector is still in the nascent stage have to be careful in protecting its development. However, the approach accepted is based on two track negotiations, one for merchandise and other for the services. The negotiations on services are being pursued on the basis of an umbrella agreement under certain principles and codes governing transperancy, non-discrimination, national treatment, access to customers, machinery for conciliation and right of withdrawal etc. According to the US proposal, the framework of negotiations for services should apply to the cross border movement of services as wall as to the establisment of foreign branches and subsidiaries for purposes of producing or delivering the services within the host country. However, the developing countries maintain that the concept of trade in services cannot be stretched to cover investment, production or distribution of services within national borders. The US proposal also seeks to impose discipline on state monopolies while ingnoring the situation pertaining to transnational corporations. There is no reference about the restrictive practices of TNCs. It further states, "Governments sometimes choose to provide services through a single monopoly entity which can either be a state enterprise or private party. The framework agreement should provide disciplines governing the behaviour of such a monopoly entity in its capacity as a sole service provider as well as in its activities when engaged in competitive services. It should also assure that appropriate compensation to affected signatories or their affacted entities is provided when a government dscides to transform the provision of a service from a compatitive to a monopoly environment. The framework should not inter fare with a government's sovsreignty to provide a service by way of a monopoly. It should, however, oblige, the monopoly entity to provide its service to foreign based users on a non-discriminatory basis with respect to price, quality and quantity."

Besides the facilities sought by the USA under National Treatment would cover equal and non-discriminatory access to the means of distribution and dalivery such as transportation and telecommunication network, access to local firms and personnel which may be critical to production and marketing of some services without being forced to form partnership. Likewise, the suggestion regarding non-discrimination is that among the signatory countries to any such agreement, the most favoured nation treatment should apply. In other words, there can be discrimination against the non-signatories. The proposal relating to the transparency measures requires not only the indction of laws and regulations, but also the need to allow examination of existing and future measures which have intended or unintended effect on access and treatment of foreign services and providers of services. The US proposal suggests that there should be prior examination of such measurss.

Evidently the position taken by the USA during the current negotiations of GATT at Geneva has grave implications for our national service sector in general and *shipping and port* sector in particular. Unlike the position in most developed countries, we have a large public sector enterprise with a sizable investment in shipping Corporation of India owning nearly 55 per cent of the national fleet. It has crucial involvement in the transport of crude oil, petroleum products, iron ore, liner cargoes to important and distant markets as well as off shore movements for oil production and exploration and island services of Andaman and Lakshdweep. Although in principle the SCI is expected to function on so called commercial principles, the socioeconomic factors and demands of administrative exigencies of the government policies, exercise considerable influence on its working. Likewise, the whols of our sea port system and sub-systems are owned and operated by the Central and the State governments. It has been so on account of the requirement of large financial investment with a long gestation period with very modest return, critical importance as a vital infrastructure for the developing economy and strategic importance on a long coastline of the country. Besides, the following aspects have to be kept in view:

1. Shipping services being inextricebly linked with trade in merchandise, 90 per cent of which moves by the searoutes, it is often used as a bargaining lever by the developed countries presently owning over 70 per cent of the world fleet. Besides, their dominance in international shipping activities results in not transfor of resourus through freight revenus sarned by dispropra-tionate carriage of trade of the developing countries. The loss of foreign exchange resources, through payment of freight bill everging 10 per cent of the value of the trade. to the developing countries may run into billions.

2. Developing countries after their liberation from the colonial rule have struggled and managed to build up their own merchant fleet, investing scarce capital resources for realising a measure of self-raliance and provide logistic support to export promotion and import facilitation. At present their share is only 15 per cent of the world fleet. They need further development of the fleet to adequately meet the growing requirement of their trade, and also to reduce the drain of foreign exchange rssources by way of payment of freight to foreign shipping lines and at the same time increase earning of foreign exchange by use of national carriers.

3. The trade boom of early seventies and the emergence of bigger and better ships on account of advances in shipbuilding technology, massive investment for expansion of shipping tonnage ensued in the developed maritime countries This was also facilitated by registration of ships in FOC countries which are tax havens. There has been also considerable amount of spaculative investment by non-shipping business groups. With the setting in, of recession in global trade which has essumed a secular character, the phenomenon of overtonnaging on an unprecedental scale has emerged. The heavy imbalance between supply of and demand for shipping services has led to cut-throat competition, much to the disadvantage of the fleets of developing countries in general and India in particular. There is virtual dumping of shipping tonnage for use in the trades of developing countries. Freight wars and use of unethical practices have become rampant, particularly in the India's overseas trade. These are detrimental to the interest of Indian shippers, shipownres and the country as a whole.

4. The situation therefore, calls for regulatory and protective measures by the Government of India for ensuring legitimate share in the carriage of our overseas trade, eradication of cut-throat rate wars and unethical business practices. Many third world countries have already

done so, both through legal as well as administrative measures. However, a free for all situation continues on the Indian coast. Consequently our share in the carriage of overseas trade has gone down to less than 20 per cent in terms of freight earnings. Nearly 50 per cent of our tonnage capacity remains unutilised and further expansion of the national fleet has stagnated. The Government of India had to write off the accumulated loss amounting to Rs. 100 crores of the Mogul Lines, one of the public sector companies at the time of its merger with Shipping Corporation of India. Scindia Steam Navigation Company with a long history of nearly 70 years is currently facing liquidation proceeding on account of losses suffered for lack of patronage by India shippers.

5. Over a period of 40 years struggle by the developing countries on the forum of UNCTAD, an international convention popularly known as Liner Code adopted in 1974 provides, for reservation of at least 40 per cent of the liner trade for providing nocassary carge base for the oparation of the nascent fleet of developing countries. For the trade in bulk cargoss, it has been agreed in principle that the developing countries with the requisite tonnage capacity have a legitimate right of carrying 50 per cent of the cargo originating or terminating within their teritories. The developing countries are now endeavouring to back out from those commitments by advancing false excuses and demand a free excess to cargo movements in the trades of developing countries, so that the excess capacity they have built-up can be utilised and their duminance in sea transport is parpetuated.

6. It has also become very convenient for the developed countries during discussions on services under the suspicious of GATT to confront the developing countries with their anti-protectionist position and demand for free market excess in the matter of merchandise trade. by proposing a trade off in the services sectar.

7. It is also a matter of serious concern that our policy approach in this rgard is not coherent and lacks consistency at international and national levels. The Government of India has not implemented the Liner Code which has come into force as early as October 1983. We are also not adequately pursuing the policy of selling CIF and buying FOB. which the public sector enterprises are strong enough to follow the retaining control over use of ships in the bulk trade. This is very much in contrsat]with the forceful stand and lead taken by our official delegations in these matters on the forum of UNCTAD, and now during the discussions on services under GATT. Apart from the damage being done to the national interest, dichotomy can erods the credibility of the purpose and intentions of the policies pursued by the Government of India.

During our discusions on trade in services under the auspices of GATT, it would be necessary to keep in view the vital issues involved in safeguarding our national interest, vis-a-vis the development of national shipping and its due share in the carriage of our overseas trade. The important points to be kapt in view in our negotiating strategy should be as foliows:

1. We should not relant or give in, on the question of securing atleast 40 per cent share in the carriage of our liner trades and 50 per cent in the bulk trades by legal or administrative means in accordance with the UNCTAD Liner Code which has come into force since October, 1983 and general consensus reached by member countries of UNCTAD for the carriage of bulk trade. We should not be taken in, by the gratuitous praise that may flow from the developed countries, for so far refraining from taking any firm actions in the form of cargo reservation for the national carriers. We should therefore, oppose any move to freeze any further protective action required to be taken by India and other developing countries for realising our objectives in the matter

of equitable sharing of cargo with our trading partners with a view to earn and save foreign exchange resources and realising some measures of selfreliance and reducing our dependence on the fleet of developed countries.

2. We should stoutly defend the bilateral shipping arrangements already entered into with USSR and other socialist countries since they are a part of the bilateral trading agreements and have operationally proved highly beneficial to the expansion of trade with them.

3. We must forcefully bring out the facts about prevalence of unfair competition, through use of unethical practices by foreign shipping lines and their agents in our trade in particular and those of the developing countries in general and continuous indulgence in dumping the excess tonnage capacity by the developed countries. This has to be eradicated if necessary through legal means for preventing drain of foreign exchange through leakage and outgo of freight revenue earned by foreign lines in an illegitimets manner when our capacity of the national fleet remains unutilised by a wide margin.

4. It is of paramount importance to develop national shipping for developing countries and particular for India for its promotional role in expansion and diversification of foreign trade ond for very vital strategic reasons for country like India with a vast coastline and its geographical location in the Indian ocean, for maintaining essential lines of supply and national defence. We should not, therefore, accept the customary argument of unnecessary use of scarce capital resources, non-viability of operations and allowing so called free access to cargoes moving in our trades. We should reiterate the policy of the Government of India enunciated on the forum of UNCTAD and emphasise that the decision reached on that forum should not be revised or nullified by the GATT round of negotiations on services.

Index

Index